ABELA
AND
HELOISE

A Play

by

RONALD MILLAR

SAMUEL FRENCH

LONDON
NEW YORK SYDNEY TORONTO HOLLYWOOD

Printed in Great Britain by W & J Mackay & Co Ltd, Chatham

ABELARD AND HELOISE

Presented by John Gale in association with Marvin Liebman and the Northcott Theatre, Exeter on 19 May 1970, at Wyndham's Theatre, London, with the following cast of characters:

Peter Abelard	*Keith Michell*
Heloise	*Diana Rigg*
Alain	*David Robb*
Gerard	*Mark Johnson*
Philippe	*Michael Mundell*
Robert de Montboissier	*Terence Wilton*
Guibert	*Philip Sayer*
Gilles de Vannes	*Timothy West*
Jehan	*Peter Sergeant*
Fulbert	*John Warner*
Belle Alys	*Valerie Minifie*
Abbess of Argenteuil	*Elspeth March*
Sister Laura	*Jo Warne*
Sister Godric	*Rosalind Atkinson*
Sister Constance	*Sandra Duncan*
Mariella	*Mary Ashton*
Gisella	*Elizabeth Norman*
Alberic of Rheims	*William Redmond*
Bernard of Clairvaux	*David Ashford*
Denise	*Jennie Stoller*
Hugh	*Stanley McGeagh*

The play directed by **Robin Phillips**

Setting by **Daphne Dare**

The action passes in France in the first half of the twelfth century

The play is inspired by "Peter Abelard" by Helen Waddele, and the letters of Abelard and Heloise.

ACT I

SCENE 1

*The Chapel of the Abbey of the Paraclete, near Troyes, France, in the year
1131 AD. An afternoon in late autumn*

*Darkness. The sound of Monks singing is heard, followed by Nuns singing. The
lighting slowly fades up. A dove, the symbol of the Holy Ghost, is seen illumin-
ated on the screen upstage. As the brightness increases, a group of Nuns and
Monks, mostly of the Benedictine order, file slowly on. The Nuns take up
positions round one tower; the Monks take up positions round the other tower.
One remains upstage holding a large wooden cross. When all are in position,
the Father Abbot and the Mother Abbess enter from opposite sides. They walk
slowly towards each other C. For a moment they face each other in silence,
then the Abbot turns away and kneels. The Abbess kneels. They pray in silence.
When the Abbot kneels, all the Monks kneel; and when the Abbess kneels, the
Nuns on the tower follow suit and the others bow their heads
The singing ends. The Abbot crosses himself, rises, and goes up the stairs of
one tower to stand by the balustrade at the top, facing the Nuns, as though in a
pulpit. As the lights come up on him, we see the Abbot clearly for the first time.
Abelard, at fifty-two, is old beyond his years. His voice is thin and soft and he
speaks slowly, his manner gentle, humble, simple. There is little to indicate the
man he was, or for that matter still is, intellectually. For here, still, is the
keenest intellect in Europe. He raises his hands. The Nuns and Monks turn
towards him. The Monks kneel. All bow their heads*

Abelard Exsurge, Domine, adiuva nos, et libera nos propter nomen tuum.
Monks and Nuns Amen. (*They raise their heads*)
Abelard Reverend Mother, Beloved Sisters in Christ, who have made the
long, hard journey across the plains of France to this, our Abbey of the
Paraclete—having been cruelly and wrongfully dispossessed of your convent in Argenteuil, we, your brothers in Christ, do herewith freely, joy-
fully and with love surrender to you this, our Abbey, with the prayer that
you may here find a refuge and a place of peace. (*He looks down at the
Abbess*) And we do name you, Reverend Mother, Beloved Sister, whose

piety, humility and devotion to God are unexampled, First Abbess of the Paraclete, for as long as you shall live. This we do in charity, before God, and in the name of his holiness Pope Innocent the second, given under his hand on the twenty-eighth of November, in the year of our Lord eleven hundred and thirty-one. And now, before we, your Brothers, take our leave of you, let us pray together for the blessing of Almighty God upon this, your new and, by God's mercy, your enduring home. Let us pray in silence.

The Nuns and Monks bow their heads. Abelard comes down the stairs and kneels. As Abelard kneels, the Nuns and Monks rise and turn upstage. We hear the silent thoughts of the Abbot and Abbess in counterpoint

(*Intimately*) Eternal Father, whose love is so strong, so deep, so ravishing that, like a crucible, it burns away down to the very marrow of the bones, all earthly love, grant to us who walk the way of the cloister that purity of soul which alone enables us to consecrate ourselves to Thee, O God our Strength and Our Redeemer.

The Mother Abbess raises her head and we see her face for the first time. Heloise is still a young woman. She is, also, still palely beautiful, the eyes as deep and haunting as ever. As she speaks, the Nuns and Monks turn downstage to look at her and raise their hands in front of them, shoulder height, palms outwards

Heloise I've never been very interested in God. These lovely, empty rituals mean less to me than one man's glance, a single touch of hands. Peter, Peter, who art here beside me, hallowed be thy name, thy will be done on earth—on earth—for what else is there?

The Nuns and Monks lower their hands. The Monks kneel, heads bowed

Abelard . . . and may Thy humble servants, Lord, proclaim the truth of Thy Gospel which says: "Love not the world, neither the things that are in the world, for all that is in the world, the lust of the flesh and the lust of the eyes, and the pride of life, is not of the Father, but of the world. And the world passeth away, and the lust thereof, but he that doeth the Will of God abideth forever."
Heloise Is this the end of the story?

The Monks and Nuns turn to look at Heloise, then turn their heads away and raise their right hands to shield their faces

Can it be that we who have known the warmth and sweetness of each other's bodies, and endured the agony of separation, have come at last together only to part again? Peter—

The Nuns drop their shielding hands and begin a low humming. The Monks drop their hands, rise, and move upstage, humming

—O my darling, love me, love me, stay with me. I think of you always, Peter. At Mass, when prayer should be purest—and alone at night, in my

cell at night, Peter, in bed, sometimes the very movements of my body—
I know it's obscene. I know that I should tremble at what I've done. I
only long for what I've lost.

The Monks halt and stop humming. The Nuns change key, humming

Do the others, too, lie sleepless in their still, cold cells, frozen into virtue?
Do they, too, long for some human nearness, to call back yesterday?

The lighting fades to a Black-out except for a spot on Heloise

The Monks, humming, file off. Abelard exits

(*With a cry*) O God, I don't belong in this spider's web of a life, with its
panic fears, it's caution, it's obsequiousness! I don't belong, you know I
don't belong!

All stop humming

I'm thirty-two. A young woman still—young and full of life. They think
me chaste, God. They call me holy. They see what I do: they can't see
what I think.

*Six Students march in two by two, downstage, marking time when they
arrive in position*

God, nothing is good save that which is done for the love of You. Isn't
that so? Well, Heloise does nothing save for the love of him in whom she
lives and moves and has her being. One name only echoes in this soul.

*The Students slap their thighs in rhythm: da-da; da-da-dah; da-da-da-da; dah
dah*

Not yours, God. O God, not yours.

*The Students clap their hands in the same rhythm and whisper "Abelard", then
continue doing this between each of Heloise's "Abelard"s and, before the last
"Abelard", stamping their feet in the same rhythm, crescendo*

Abelard! Abelard, Abelard, Abelard . . .

The light fades on Heloise and she exits   1*

SCENE 2

Outside Abelard's lodgings in Paris. Some fifteen years earlier

*The voice of Heloise melts into the voices of the young male Students, who
move downstage, cheering and shouting, as two of their number bear Abelard
shoulder high to his lodgings. He is deposited triumphantly at the top of the*

* See Production Plot, page 75.

steps to further cheers and cries of "Speech! Speech, Master! Speech!".
*Abelard, at thirty-seven, Master of the Schools at Notre Dame, is at the peak
of his powers and entirely aware of the fact. The voice we now hear is strong
and vibrant and he is dressed with considerable elegance. Apart from the
tonsured head, there is nothing of the cleric about him. He looks down at the
students clustered round the steps with the amused tolerance of a man whose
audience is, in every sense, at his feet. The cries of* "Speech" *are renewed*

Abelard No, no, gentlemen. No more speeches.

A groan of disappointment goes up

No, I'm sorry, but two lectures a day is enough. Besides, I'm dry.
Alain (*a student*) Master, what's your opinion . . .
Abelard I'm also hungry, and when the body calls the mind must wait.
Thank you for the ride. (*He waves and turns to go up*)
Alain Just one question, Master. Should a priest marry?

There is a murmur from the Students. They know what is coming

Abelard (*turning back in surprise*) I thought it was philosophy we were
studying, gentlemen.
Alain Yes, sir, but philosophically speaking, sir—the tonsure being a
symbol of continence—well, you *are* an expert, aren't you, sir?
Abelard On priests or marriage?
Alain On continence—you being a member of the celibate community, sir,
and—well, I was wondering . . .
Abelard (*putting a hand on Alain's shoulder*) Tell me, Alain, which are you
planning to enter first, the Church or matrimony?

Laughter

Second Student It's not Alain, sir. It's Canon Evrard.
Abelard Evrard?
Third Student Haven't you heard, Master?
Philippe It's all over Paris, sir.
Third Student Canon Evrard has married his housekeeper, sir.
Abelard (*after a pause; mildly*) Then I suggest you take your question to the
Canon. Better still, look up your Theophrastus. He's excellent on marriage
in general and wives in particular. Good day, gentlemen.
Students Theophrastus? Tell us about Theophrastus, sir! Go on, Master!
Tell us, Master! etc.
Abelard (*turning back good-humouredly*) Well then—but briefly. No yoke
bears heavier on a man than marriage. To feed a poor wife is a burden;
to support a rich one, torment. For if she's beautiful, men run after her,
and if she's ugly she runs after men.

Laughter

So that a man has either to keep what everyone wants or what no one
wants. In short, says Theophrastus, a life devoted to the study of truth
can't be shared with a woman, it's too exhausting. So if you would serve
philosophy, gentlemen, don't take a wife: get a good servant!

Laughter

Gerard Or a good mistress.

Laughter

Abelard (*seriously*) No. No, if you must love, love reason. The world is sloughing off the skin of centuries slowly. It likes nothing better than to live like a pig in a sty. (*Powerfully*) Goad the porkers. Quicken dead minds. If you love reason, awaken thought. If you love reason, accept nothing blindly. If you love reason, probe, challenge, question the unquestionable. And if you love me, for God's sake go home and let me have my dinner. (*He goes up the stairs*)

Laughter

Third Student Good night, Master.

With general "Good night"*s the Students drift off, all except one, Robert*

Robert Master!
Abelard Well, a new face. What's your name, boy?
Robert Robert, sir. Robert de Montbossier.
Abelard Student?
Robert Novice monk. On leave from Cluny, Master.
Abelard A monk from Cluny? I know it well.
Robert I *was* at Clairvaux. I left Clairvaux for Cluny.
Abelard No one who knows Clairvaux will blame you for that.
Robert It's a cold place, Clairvaux. Cold.
Abelard And Bernard of Clairvaux even colder. But now you've left Cluny also. Why?
Robert To attend the Schools. To hear Master Abelard lecture at Notre Dame.
Abelard I trust the course is proving instructive?
Robert The greatest experience of my life. I try to take down every lecture—when you don't go too fast for me—and memorize it afterwards. "It is our custom in our daily speech to speak of things as they appear to our eyes"—that's my favourite.
Abelard (*correcting him*) "Senses. It is our custom in our daily speech to speak of things as they appear to our *senses*, rather than as they are in actual fact. For example, we say it's a starry sky, or not, or that the moon is shining more, or less, or even not at all, when these things, however variable they seem to us, are in fact changeless."
Robert I'd never thought of it like that. Through your eyes, it—it's a new world.
Abelard I'm flattered. But tell me, boy, do you always swallow what your teacher tells you?
Robert It depends on the teacher. Abelard is the greatest in all France.
Abelard (*sharply*) In all Europe.
Robert He alone teaches the faith of reason. He alone offers a coherent view of God. He alone heats the soul and lights the mind. He alone . . .

Abelard Yes, quite. Quite. Of course, it's conceivable—though naturally improbable—that he could, just once in a while, be wrong?
Robert No, sir. Never. Not Abelard.
Abelard I'm bound to say I agree with you. Nevertheless—little monk, I have a shock for you . . .

Guibert, Abelard's servant, enters

Guibert It's on the table, Master.
Abelard I'm coming, Guibert.
Guibert I've made you a nice omelette.

Guibert exits

Abelard I have a shock for you. Prepare yourself. Abelard is not God.
Robert Sometimes I think so.
Abelard (*not displeased*) Yes, I thought you did, you blasphemous pup. They'd flog you for that at Clairvaux or Cluny. Not God, Robert. The best available alternative, possibly. In fact, almost certainly. But not God.

The lights fade. To cover the scene change Students are heard singing "The Abbot of Angers".

SCENE 3

Gilles' room in the lee of Notre-Dame   **2**

Gillies de Vannes enters and sits at the table. He is a Canon and is seventy years of age. He sits in his great chair, his massive chin creased on his chest. On the table is a partly eaten chicken and a flagon of wine and two goblets. As the lights come up Abelard enters.

Abelard Don't get up.
Gilles I wasn't intending to. Sciatica.
Abelard I thought it was better.
Gilles (*with a grunt*) I suppose you've come for your dinner?

(He throws a chicken leg at Abelard)

Abelard (*catching it*) Well, since you press me. My man Guibert made me an omelette. The grease stood on it in flakes. I don't know why his food always tastes so foul. He washes the platters, even the pots.
Gilles But does he wash the cloth that washes the pots? There's no flavour quite like it.
Abelard It's lack of concentration, I think. His mind is on women. (*Eating*) This chicken is delicious.
Gilles From my cousin, the Abbess, at Argenteuil. Why do nuns always have the best poultry?

Abelard Plump white flesh. Cluck-cluck-cluck. (*He eats ravenously*)

Gilles (*chuckling*) It's a pleasure to feed you, Peter. Not only because you eat like a hungry hawk, but because, like me, you're a sensualist.

Abelard (*with his mouth full*) God forbid.

Gilles It's true. But I'm a sensualist in mind as well as body. Your mind snuffs up the east wind, which is why you're as lean as the kine of Pharaoh. But there's hope for you. I was once as lean as you—*and* fasted more often, till I was past grace.

Abelard I've sometimes wondered if you ever knew it. (*He starts to fill the goblets*)

Gilles Grace? (*He holds out his goblet*)

Abelard pours a drop into it

To the brim.

Abelard fills Gilles' goblet, then his own

Oh yes, I knew it. But—is it Jerome or Ambrose? "Nothing so estrangeth the heart from the love of God as the faces of women."

Abelard Not Jerome.

Gilles No. Too crude. The Blessed Gregory, perhaps. And after that, there was this. (*Raising his goblet*) Was that hullabaloo this morning your students?

Abelard A few high spirits.

Gilles I hear they carried you shoulder high.

Abelard They may have thought of putting me in the Seine. But they set me instead on my own doorstep.

Gilles Where, naturally, you made them a speech.

Abelard I may have said a few words.

Gilles On reason as the habitation of God with men?

Abelard We arrived there eventually.

Gilles John Scotus Erigena said the same thing three hundred years ago. They killed him for it in the end, you know. Stabbed him to death with their pens. Like Hypatia. Which reminds me, Fulbert's niece is back from the convent.

Abelard Fulbert has relatives? I always thought he happened spontaneously.

Gilles There was a brother, killed in the Crusades. He sired a daughter. She borrows my Homer.

Abelard Odd taste for a girl.

Gilles Oh, Heloise has a mind. One reason, among many, why her uncle dotes on her.

Abelard Does he? (*Leaning interestedly forward*) Incestuously?

Gilles My dear Peter . . .

Abelard No, I suppose not. Tedious old sheep.

Gilles You have said that, I think, about every one of our Canons, barring myself.

Abelard Well, so they are. Sheep, every one of them browsing over the same close-bitten pastures, with their "Saint this saith that" and "Saint

that saith the other" and "Saint the other saith something else again".
As if one couldn't prove anything, and deny it, and prove it back again,
out of Augustine alone. One day I'll do it, just to show them.

Gilles Do what?

Abelard Smash the whole blind system of theology and substitute . . .

Gilles Master Peter Abelard?

Abelard Not that. Not that. But a reasonable soul. Augustine said a man
should serve the *understanding* of things. I'll be content if when I'm dead
someone says that about me. That's why these youngsters like me, you
know. There's a natural reasonable soul in most things when they're
young. I can do what I please with them.

Gilles The young, yes. But have a care for the sheep, Peter. Old teeth still
bite.

*Canon Fulbert fusses in. An aged and excitable ecclesiastic, as thin and
spiderish as Gilles is fat and florid, there is something naïve and childlike
about him. He is in full canonicals*

Fulbert (*to Gilles*) Ah, there you are, Canon. All is in order. All is in order.
Is Heloise not here yet? (*Suddenly seeing Abelard*) Oh, Master Peter.
(*He shakes Abelard's hand*) An honour, sir. An honour, as always. Yes,
indeed. I sent my niece to the library for a . . . (*To Gilles*) You're not
dressed.

Gilles Not dressed? Am I naked?

Fulbert Not dressed, not dressed for the deprivation!

Abelard (*sharply*) Deprivation?

Fulbert Yes, yes, yes, the deprivation of Evrard! Hurry, man, we don't
want to be late. It promises to be something of an occasion.

Gilles You may go your ways, Fulbert. Not one foot will you get me inside
the Cathedral tonight.

Fulbert What? Now listen to me, de Vannes, you gave your word . . .

Gilles And don't wag your finger at me. What does the man look like?
A wasp attacking a porcupine.

Fulbert (*stiffly*) I confess I find some difficulty in comprehending your
position, de Vannes. You gave your vote with the rest of us in Chapter.

Gilles I did.

Fulbert And yet you refuse . . .

Gilles But I have no liking for executions of justice. A bad conscience, no
doubt.

Fulbert Evrard is a Canon, not a choirboy. And a simple act of ecclesiastical
deprivation . . .

Gilles —is something I choose not to witness. Oh, he's been a fool, I grant
you. If he'd made her his mistress instead of his wife, we'd have looked the
other way in charity.

Fulbert *I* would not have looked the other way!

Gilles It's normal practice.

Fulbert It's hypocrisy.

Gilles Well, of course.

Fulbert I deplore it. A priest is a servant of God. Thou canst not serve God and woman.

Gilles (*to Abelard*) You hear that, Peter? Fulbert has unearthed the Eleventh Commandment.

Fulbert You mock me, Gilles.

Gilles There, there, you're a good fellow, Fulbert. A thorn in the flesh of the unrighteous. But I will not go to your entertainment.

Fulbert I like a friend to sit with.

Gilles Ask Abelard. Perhaps he'll go with you and hold your hand.

Fulbert (*eagerly*) Master Peter? It would be a considerable honour. I'm in need of a friend.

Abelard It's Evrard, I think, who needs the friend. I'll see you there.

Abelard goes out abruptly

Fulbert (*plaintively*) Why wouldn't he walk with me, why didn't he wait?

One of the bells of Notre-Dame starts to toll

I'm to make your excuses, then, Gilles?

Gilles Tell them I have a profound sciatica.

Fulbert Have you?

Gilles No, but I had yesterday.

Fulbert T't, Heloise, where is the girl? I shall be late. I sent her to the Library for a copy of *The Fathers*—on illicit union within the Church— in case our brother contests the decision, you understand. But it shouldn't take her more than five minutes. If something has happened to her—some dreadful disaster—

Gilles No, no, no.

Fulbert—I shall never forgive myself.

Gilles Too much excitement is bad for the heart, Fulbert. Think of your heart.

Fulbert There's nothing wrong with my heart.

Gilles Then think of mine.

Heloise runs in, breathless. She wears green, girdled low, her long hair falling to her shoulders. The eyes are haunting. She is seventeen. She kisses Fulbert and hands him a book

Fulbert There you are child. Where on earth have you been?

Heloise I'm sorry, Uncle. I ran both ways all the way.

Fulbert In that case I can't imagine why it took you so long.

Heloise kisses Gilles

Now you'll go straight home, sweetheart?

Heloise Yes.

Gilles Leave her with me, Fulbert, while you're in Chapter. There's a copy of the inscription for the lapidaries to make and I've gout in my thumb.

Fulbert You think the girl writes well, Gilles?

Gilles She has the best clerk's script in Paris.

Fulbert Beauty—and a brain to match.

Gilles A rare combination for some unfortunate man.

Fulbert No. Heloise is mine—and God's. (*He places his hand on Heloise's head*)

Gilles I notice you place God below the salt.

Fulbert I will come back for her when Chapter is over. And then I can tell you, Canon, all about it.

Gilles I can scarcely contain myself, Canon. Oh, and Fulbert—I would come with you to the stoning of Stephen, if I had the courage.

Fulbert (*kindly*) Not Stephen. Evrard. (*Aside to Heloise*) He's getting old.

Fulbert goes out

Gilles and Heloise look at each other and burst out laughing

Gilles (*pouring out wine*) Heloise, you're the only contemporary I have.

Heloise I think so, too. Where are the inscriptions?

Gilles An excuse for your company. (*Offering her his goblet*) Here, try this.

Heloise Mn. Cold and green like well-water—(*She drinks*)—yet it warms like the sun. (*She gives Gilles his goblet, then takes one and pours wine for herself*) Where does it come from?

The bell ceases tolling

Gilles Moselle. Isn't it strange that a man with a palate like Ausonius should write a long poem about that dull river and not one line about its vineyards?

Heloise Perhaps he despised them, being from Bordeaux.

Gilles A man's palate should have no country.

Heloise Gilles, what will become of Evrard? Was he wrong to marry?

Gilles Canonically, yes.

Heloise Then is marriage a sin?

Gilles Not a sin. Only a mistake.

She grins

That's why the canonists regard it so gravely. One can be absolved of a sin, but there's no absolution for a mistake.

Heloise But Evrard—it was such a good face, and she—I saw his wife this morning at her door, all sodden with crying and frightened.

Gilles God comfort her in her distress.

Heloise My uncle says you voted against Evrard in Chapter.

Gilles And should vote again tomorrow.

Heloise But why, Gilles? You, of all people? *You're* not a hypocrite.

Gilles But I am. Officially I'm a Canon of Notre-Dame, and I have the morals, and, what's worse, the appearance of Silenus.

Heloise At least you make no pretence at goodness, like the others. Yet you condemned Evrard.

Gilles Canon law condemned him, as it would condemn the Archbishop if charges against him were brought and proved. And marriage, remember, is easier to prove than—other forms of depravity.

Heloise Is that how you think of marriage? As a form of depravity?

Gilles Marriage—is a compromise with the flesh. The Church in its wisdom has given its blessing to that compromise, speaking of a certain spiritual union, of which I have seen little and desired less. To me the root of marriage is the satisfying of a lust of the flesh.

Heloise Then love is lust?

Gilles Its root is lust. You find that horrible.

Heloise (*almost inaudibly*) Yes.

Gilles (*gently*) The rose is lovelier than its root, Heloise. Even so, marriage is the effort to make that permanent which is by nature transient. Nequidquam. In vain.

Abelard enters

So soon? That was a swift stoning. What happened? Did they all throw at once? You've not met, I think. Heloise—the man who has your generation by the ears—Master Peter Abelard.

Abelard (*after a moment*) I've just come from your uncle. He fainted in Chapter. There's no cause for concern. He'd been fasting, I think. He asks you should go to him.

Heloise (*quickly*) Yes, of course. (*She gives the goblet to Gilles and moves upstage*)

Abelard (*following her*) I'll see you there safely.

Heloise No. Thank you, but I—I'll be quicker alone.

Heloise runs out

Abelard stares after her

Gilles (*rising*) Seventeen, they say. Not much colour.

As he speaks, Gilles moves downstage with Abelard. The Nuns take up a position to watch the following scene. **3**

Alys and Alain enter, go up the tower and embrace. Guibert enters

I like a white-faced wench myself. The eyes show better so. Why do fools say black as night? There's more colour in a night sky than ever there is at noonday. Stars, too. You're not listening.

A spot comes up on Guibert, and a treble solo voice is heard singing "When summer on is stealing"

Abelard I'm listening.

Guibert Alys!

Abelard My man Guibert—in search of woman.

Gilles (*chuckling*) Ah, yes.

Abelard and Gilles exit

SCENE 4

Outside a house in the poor quarter of Paris. Moonlight

The lighting comes up on Alain and Alys. Alain comes down in high satisfaction adjusting his clothes

Alain (*calling up to Alys*) Hey! Alys!

Alys leans out

Thanks!

Alys (*a tart, but comely*) Pleasure, dear. Come again.

Alain That I will.

Alys Any time. I'm all yours.

Alain exits
Robert crosses

I'm all yours too, dear.

Robert glances up, then hurries off

Please yourself. (*She starts to withdraw*)

Guibert lumbers out of the shadows

Guibert (*hoarsely*) Alys! Alys! Don't go!

Alys Who's there? Oh, it's you, Guibert. Got any money?

Guibert Is it money tonight, Alys?

Alys Money every night, dear. I'm not in this for the timbrels and dancing.

Guibert I've got a new song.

Alys Can't eat songs, dear.

Guibert You liked the one I sang you last week—remember? And then—afterwards, Oh, Alys, it was so wonderful.

The singing finishes

Alys Yes, well, you got the better of my good nature. There's been a change of policy. (*She starts to withdraw*)

Guibert No, wait! Alys. Listen! (*He sings*)

When Summer on is stealing,

Alys moves to listen

And come the gracious prime
And Phoebus high in heaven
And fled the rime

Guibert sits

With love of one young maiden
My heart hath ta'en its wound
And manifold the grief that I
In love have found
That I in love have found.

Alys slowly comes down and stands behind Guibert

> If she would once have pity
> And take me to her side
> And stooping lean down o'er me
> And so abide,
> And stooping lean down o'er me

Alys fondles his head

> And so abide.

Abelard enters and moves into the shadows to watch the ensuing scene

Alys Who wrote that?
Guibert I did.
Alys Liar.
Guibert Well, it's one of Master Abelard's, actually. One of his best, don't you think?
Alys Not bad. (*She stands invitingly before him*)
Guibert (*moving hesitantly to her*) Can I come in now?

Alys puts up her mouth. He kisses her hungrily. She responds

Alys (*eventually*) There. Now go on home like a good little boy.
Guibert But—but, Alys, we haven't . . .
Alys I said go home.
Guibert Oh, God. Please—please—I must—I must . . . (*He seizes her clumsily*)

She wrestles and throws him off. He sprawls on the ground

Alys (*without rancour*) No free rides. I'm a business girl.
Guibert (*rising*) How much?
Alys How long?
Guibert All night?

Alys gives a derisive laugh

All night, Alys?
Alys You bring me a hundred gold besants, you can have me for a night.
Guibert A hundred gold besants?
Alys That's what I said.
Guibert Just for one night?
Alys 'Course, if I'm not worth it . . .
Guibert Yes—(*surveying her hungrily*)—God, yes, you're worth it. But where am I going to get a hundred besants?
Alys That's your problem, isn't it, dear? And look—Guibert—don't bother me again. Not unless you've solved it. All right?
Guibert Alys, for God's sake . . .
Alys Oh, go home!

Alys exits

Guibert moves downstage   **4**

Guibert (*to the audience*) I'll get it. A hundred gold besants. I don't know
how, but I'll get it. Once you've had a woman, well, you know how
it is . . .

Abelard appears out of the shadows

Abelard No, I don't know how it is.
Guibert No, that's right, Master. Nor you would.
Abelard But I can imagine. The hunger. The hunger for love.
Guibert That's it, sir. That's it, exactly. (*He snaps his fingers*) I'll save.
That's it. I'll start saving.
Abelard (*opening a purse at his waist and handing Guibert a coin*) To open
your account.
Guibert Thanks, Master Abelard. That's—sympathetic.

Guibert exits

SCENE 5

Abelard's old room in Paris

Abelard moves below the bench   **5**

Abelard (*to the audience*) A scullion and a harlot—and yet—when she
took him in her arms and their mouths met, it seemed to me as if suddenly
all the things that I contend for—books, philosophy, dialectics—

Gilles enters

—the whole spectrum of the intellectual life—as if suddenly they were
nothing. It was as though—for a moment in time—harlot and lout had—
immortality. Can you believe that, Gilles?
Gilles (*moving to the chair and sitting*) Without difficulty. And then?
Abelard And then she slapped his face and shut the door on him.
Gilles Ha! Yes, that's the way of it. Poor Guibert. By the way, Fulbert
says you can take him with you. Yvonne, that's his cook, will be happy
to feed you, but naturally you must have a man about you to fetch and
carry.
Abelard (*sharply*) What's this?
Gilles Fulbert wants you to go and live with him.
Abelard *Fulbert* wants *me* . . .?
Gilles The picture of stupefaction. Now why?
Abelard Why? Good God, man . . .
Gilles He was always by way of regarding you as a demigod, and since you
carried him home when he fainted in Chapter . . .
Abelard I did not. I gave him an arm.
Gilles Horizontal or vertical, the fact remains he blushes and stammers

whenever he speaks of you. Which is why I am Winged Mercury—well, scarcely winged, but none the less a messenger.

Abelard I don't understand anything you're saying.

Gilles Apparently there's a room at the top of the house. It looks over the Seine. An improvement, I gather, on your present quarters. Well, almost anything would be that. There's space enough for yourself and your books, and he'll take you for half what your housekeeping costs you now, but he asks, with diffidence, if in part consideration of board and lodging, you would, in such leisure as your weightier studies afford you, instruct his niece. He bade me say that she'll be at your disposal whenever you choose. (*He heaves with silent laughter*)

Abelard Is the man out of his wits? I'm thirty-seven and she's . . .

Gilles A schoolgirl. I reminded him of the fact, but he spoke much of your reputation for chastity, and of St Jerome and his pupil Eustochium. You would, it seems, be doing him the greatest imaginable honour if you would consent to live under his roof.

Abelard Honour?

Gilles His word. He used it at least three times. Well? Is it to be yes or no?

Abelard Tell me.

Gilles My good Peter, I'm the last person on earth to ask that question of. Never in my life have I said no to anything I greatly desired. But then—you already have the male population at your feet—perhaps you've never really wanted—anything else?

Abelard (*after a moment*) Yes, once. One summer I went home to my father's house at Le Palais, to my sister Denise. She married Hugh, my father's steward. And I'd have given all I had to be like Hugh and sweat all the mischief out of me at the hay and then go back and lie all night with something warm and kind like Denise.

The Nuns whisper "Heloise"

And I could have cursed my wits that had spoiled me for living. And my head—God, how it ached! And then Denise would come and sit beside me on the grass and hold my head in her hands. No woman had ever done that to me.

Gilles Ah, those hands, those healing woman's hands—that moment when they take your head in their hands and carry it to their breasts . . .

The lights fade. Gilles exits

SCENE 6

Abelard's room in Fulbert's house. June

It is a comfortably furnished room at the top of the house. Nothing luxurious, but an obvious improvement on his previous lodgings.

The Monks move away upstage on one side, and the Nuns move up on   **6** *the other. Fulbert enters unnoticed during the general movement and joins Abelard*

Fulbert . . . You'll find she has a good mind, a logical mind. And an
excellent memory. Whatever you teach her, she'll retain. Stores it all up
here, she does, like a—whatever animal never forgets. I forget. Now, you
have everything you require? Splendid. And we have your man—what's
his name?—
Abelard Guibert.
Fulbert—Guibert installed in the loft, so all is in order. All is in order.
(*He calls*) Heloise! Come along up, my dear. She'll prove an apt pupil,
a worthy pupil, I have no doubt. If not, you must punish her. Yes,
indeed. A touch of the birch on the buttocks is good for all of us,
especially the young.

Heloise enters

A thing they know well in convents—the value of a touch of the birch
about our hinder parts—isn't that so, my dear? Mind you, the nuns
thought highly of her. A devout girl, pious and virtuous, neither the
desires nor the vanities of this world could turn her from her studies. A
natural religious, I should say. But I'm wasting your precious time. (*To
Heloise*) It's a privilege to have such an eminent man give a few hours
to a child like you. Remember that. (*He gives her a little kiss*) Master
Peter, I place my niece in your hands. Confidently. Without reserve.
You are a great man of letters. My house is honoured. Yes, indeed.

*Fulbert gives a little half-bow, clears his throat, and shuffles out on his
walking-stick*

Abelard (*at length; coldly*) Sit down.

Heloise sits obediently

(*Eventually*) Did the nuns beat you?
Heloise No. (*After a pause*) I think they preferred to beat themselves.
Abelard (*after a pause*) They say it sharpens the soul.
Heloise (*thoughtfully*) I don't think it would sharpen mine. In fact, I'm
sure it wouldn't. (*She pauses*) But then I've never tried it.
Abelard No doubt that will come later.

She smiles up at him. He makes no attempt to lighten his expression

You like Homer, I believe?
Heloise I've read the *Iliad* and the *Odyssey*.
Abelard What did you make of them?
Heloise (*warmly*) Oh, Homer. Homer was inspired, wasn't he?
Abelard I doubt if the point has been disputed. (*After a pause*) Is that all
you have to say about Homer?
Heloise Weren't his poems the dawn of reason?
Abelard Not the dawn. But a beacon fire. The cry of the watchman; the
dawn is coming. It was four hundred years later, when Buddha appeared
in India, Confucius in China, Plato and Aristotle in Greece, that man

began at last to break the chains that bind him to the animal. The heat is stifling. Do you mind? (*He moves as if opening a window*)

Heloise I love the breeze from the river.

Abelard (*after a pause*) What Latin have you?

Heloise I've studied the Fathers—Jerome, Gregory, Augustine. Some Ovid. A little Seneca.

Abelard Seneca?

Heloise I read *Medea* at night with my uncle.

Abelard (*after a pause*) You're seventeen?

Heloise And a half.

Abelard And you spend your evenings reading Seneca with your uncle?

Heloise When he's not too tired. He often is, which is why I suggested— you see, the house was too large for just the two of us and Yvonne in the kitchen—and when Gilles de Vannes happened to mention that you were unhappy in your lodgings . . .

Abelard (*staring at her*) Do I understand that—that this—that my coming here was *your* idea?

Heloise I'm sure you'll find it more comfortable. Did you know you can see four of the city gates from this window? And the Seine valley away to the right stretching for more than twenty miles. Paris is so lovely. Sometimes the sheer beauty of it catches the breath. Is something the matter?

Abelard (*rapt*) I'm sorry. You were saying?

Heloise Just that Paris is beautiful. There's a sort of—inner radiance.

There is a pause

Abelard (*abruptly*) Yes. There's also a stench of foul water and the drains defy description. We'll start with Virgil.

She moves eagerly

But not now. In a week—two weeks—a month, perhaps. If I have time. You understand, I have very little time.

She smiles at him. The lights fade.

SCENE 7

The same. Another day. July   7

Heloise is translating to Abelard

Abelard "Omne adeo genus in terrs hominumque ferarumque—"

Heloise "Thus every race on earth of men and beasts—"

Abelard "Et genus aequoreum—"

Heloise "And the creatures of the sea—"

Abelard "Pecudes pictaeque volucres—"

Heloise "The cattle—"
Abelard "Herds."
Heloise "The herds—and birds of brilliant hue—"
Abelard "In furias ignemque ruunt—"
Heloise "Are swept with fiery feelings—"
Abelard "Passion."
Heloise "Are swept with passion."
Abelard "Amor omnibus idem."
Heloise "Love is the same for all."
Abelard Good. (*He closes the Virgil*) That will do for today.
Heloise Of course, it's not true, is it?
Abelard What is not true?
Heloise Love is not the same for all. How can it be?
Abelard You have the advantage of me.
Heloise To love God, for example, is not the same as to love—another human being.
Abelard (*after a moment*) Which would you say is the greater love?

All the Monks and Nuns turn to stare down at Abelard and Heloise

Heloise The nuns would say "to love God".
Abelard What do *you* say? (*Before she can reply*) If you have the smallest doubt about the answer, you should certainly think twice before taking the veil.
Heloise (*astonished*) Taking the veil? But I've never considered such a step!
Abelard (*equally astonished*) I understood from your uncle . . .
Heloise (*laughing*) No, no, no. Oh, you mustn't believe all my uncle says; he's like a child at times. I have no vocation. None whatever. Taking the veil—that's just an escape, isn't it?
Abelard Most people would call it a dedication,
Heloise I've always thought of it as an escape.
Abelard From what?
Heloise A sordid world to a saintly one. But only for those who want to be saints.
Abelard If you can be happy in it, it's considered the nearest thing to heaven.
Heloise I couldn't. I couldn't be happy in it. To me it would be like being locked in a cupboard. And anyway, I don't find the world sordid I find it beautiful—and unexpected. And to have to learn to crush the desire for—for all that's most desirable—I don't believe we were given feelings simply to suppress them. Oh, they were kind and dear to me at Argenteuil and I think of them always with affection, but the room where the beggars came and waited for the almoner smelt of unwashed rags, and the bunch of herbs that hung from the ceiling was black with dead flies. Sometimes I felt as if everyone there was in love with death. Not Sister Godric, who's Irish, or Reverend Mother, who drinks, but everyone else, except the novices. I could never be a nun. Never.

The lights fade. The Nuns and Monks whisper "Abelard" four times

SCENE 8

The same. Early evening of another day. August

The pupil-teacher relationship has all but vanished

Abelard The priesthood? No, I'm too much of a rebel. Reason can't breathe in the cloister.

Heloise But there's no advancement for a man outside the Church. And you'd soon be a bishop, and then an archbishop, and then a cardinal, and then . . .

Abelard (*amused*) His Holiness?

Heloise Why not? You already have the haircut.

Abelard laughs

I'm serious. Didn't Plato say it would be well for that state whose king was a philosopher?

Abelard Yes, he did, but . . .

Heloise So what of Christendom if a philosopher were Pope? Oh, with your intellect, your energy, your sway over people, I just know you could reach the highest office.

Abelard My dear child . . .

Heloise (*sharply*) Don't call me that!

Abelard Be glad to be young, Heloise. Nothing lasts.

Heloise I thought only the old made those remarks.

Abelard (*mildly*) There *are* twenty years between us.

Heloise Is that how you see yourself? As old?

Abelard How do you see me?

Heloise As a man in his prime.

Abelard And you—you are at the spring-time.

They are suddenly very still, very aware. He makes to touch her hair, then withdraws his hand

It's just twenty years—I was seventeen—when I clattered down the track from Le Palais and made my way to Paris, with but one thought in my mind—my love of learning—and but one desire—to give all my might to letters. Yes, I'm content to teach.

Heloise Is that what you've most wanted all your life? To be a teacher?

Abelard I think what I most wanted was to be free—open to the world. At any rate, that was why I refused to be knighted and go and play the squire at Clisson.

Heloise What happened?

Abelard My father sent my brother instead.

Heloise Was he furious with you?

Abelard I never had a hard word from my father. He was more of a saint than any man I ever knew. It was Mother who gave us what chiding we got, which was little enough. She took the veil at Poitiers two months after he entered at Saint Savin. It's not the worst end, to have served in the wars and taken a wife and begotten children and then at the last to take down one's sail and ride at anchor in God.

Heloise (*softly*) Could that be the way for you?

Abelard (*suddenly restless*) I hate to be tied. The light's going. I'll get the candles.

Heloise No, don't. It's such a night. Let's just wait and watch the darkness. It's breathtaking, isn't it, Paris at night. Like a great ship, high on the water. I never knew my mother. Tell me about yours.

Abelard She had the most beautiful eyes. Not just lovely. Loveliness is an easy thing. Most women have something of it when they're young. But beauty—one, perhaps two in a generation.

Heloise And are they happy?

Abelard Happy? What do they want with happiness? They know ecstasy. (*Moving very near her*) Happiness? A dog asleep in the sun. A dog——asleep . . .

Suddenly she is in his arms and the words are lost as he kisses her mouth, her eyes, her throat. The daylight is almost gone. He breaks. She looks up at him, shaken, afraid—but with love

Heloise (*in a whisper*) Peter . . . ?

Abelard turns blindly away and goes out

Trembling, in wonder, she speaks his name

Peter . . .

The lights fade, The Monks and Nuns whisper "Peter" several times, like an echo

SCENE 9

Gilles' room. Morning   8

Heloise is standing alone.

Gilles (*off*) Push, boy, push! Where's your energy? What have you been doing all night?

Gilles is wheeled on towards Heloise by his servant, Jehan

I apologize for receiving you like this.

Jehan goes out and returns with a tray, jug of wine and goblet

Heloise You look very handsome. But should you be sitting up? Jehan says your sciatica . . .

Gilles I shall die sitting up. I will not have him pour my soup over my face as if he were manuring rhubarb. (*To Jehan*) Bring the Moselle.

Heloise Not for me.

Gilles For me, for me.

Jehan Master Simon said you wasn't to drink.

Gilles Tell Master Simon I had sciatica and drank myself out of it when he was cutting his first tooth.

Heloise (*reading from the Book of Psalms*) "Whither shall I go from thy spirit or whither shall I flee from they presence?"

Gilles (*to Jehan*) Here, give it to me. (*He takes the flagon and goblet from Jehan and pours himself a drink*)

Jehan puts the tray down and exits

Heloise "If I ascend up into Heaven, thou art there: if I make my bed in Hell, behold thou art there. If I take the wings of the morning, and dwell in the uttermost parts of the sea, even there shall thy hand lead me, and thy right hand shall hold me." (*She snaps the book shut, tense*) Not much use in going away, then. (*She drops the book on a chair*)

Gilles (*watching her*) Do you want to go away?

Heloise I need time. Where can I go?

Gilles That's easy enough. It's the Eve of St Michael. I shall send Jehan to Argenteuil—his sister's husband runs the ferry—with an offering for tomorrow's feast and greetings to my cousin the Abbess. You can ride pillion behind him and come back with him this evening.

Heloise Or not.

Gilles Don't you want to come back?

Heloise I don't know. I shan't know—until I've gone.

Gilles (*after a pause*) Where is your uncle?

Heloise At Mass.

Gilles Run back and get your cloak. I shall tell him the Sisters were grieved at being neglected all summer and that I urged you to go and make amends.

Heloise You'll lie for me?

Gilles Truth has as many coats as an onion—and each one a puzzle when you peel it.

Heloise Two minutes with you—and nothing matters as much as one thinks it does. (*She hugs him*)

Gilles (*with a yelp of agony*) Jesus, Mary and Joseph!

Heloise (*springing up*) What is it?

Gilles My hip! My hip!

Heloise Oh God! I forgot. Shall I rub it for you?

Gilles (*roaring*) *Rub* it? I'd sooner be broken on the wheel. Away with you, girl, away with you!

Heloise turns to go

Wait! (*Holding out the wine bottle*) Take this to the Abbess. She's drinking herself to death but she has my palate and we de Vannes are hard to kill. Though I'm not sure you haven't done for this one. (*He lies back and groans*)

Heloise Are you certain you wouldn't like me to . . .
Gilles Out! Out! For pity's sake, out!!

The lights fade

Heloise exits and Jehan wheels Gilles away in his chair.

SCENE 10

The Convent at Argenteuil   9

When the lights come up, the Nuns are revealed at prayer, singing. The Mother Abbess faces them. She is as massive as Gilles, and deep voiced.

Nuns   Deus in adjutorium meum intende
                            Domine ad adjuvandum me festina
                            Gloria Patri et Filio et Spiritui Sancto

The Nuns kneel

                            Sicut erat in pincipio et nunc et semper et in secula
                            seculorum.
                            Amen!

Mother Abbess (*spoken*) And now to God the Father, God the Son, and God the Holy . . .

There is a gentle tinkling of the Convent Bell. The Mother Abbess breaks off. Two Nuns' heads come up

(*Firmly*) . . . And God the Holy Ghost—

The heads go instantly down

—be ascribed, as is most justly due, all might, majesty, dominion and power, now and for evermore.
Nuns (*singing*) Amen!

The bell rings again. The Nuns rise. The Mother Abbess nods to Sister Laura, who moves to the grill   10

Sister Laura Ave Maria purissima.
Heloise (*off*) Conceived without sin.
Sister Laura (*peering into the shadows*) Blessed Virgin! Look who's here! My dear, my dear, come in, come in.

Sister Laura goes and brings in Heloise who carries a bottle under her cloak

The Mother Abbess comes forward, followed discreetly by the Nuns. Heloise drops to her knees and kisses the Abbess's ring, then rises

Abbess Well, child. (*She kisses Heloise*) You're a sight for sore eyes. I was for giving you a good scolding, but I've no mind for it now. How did you come?

Heloise I rode behind Jehan, Reverend Mother. Master Gilles was sending him with offerings for the Feast tomorrow and he—I begged to come, too.

Abbess And where is Jehan?

Heloise Gone to his sister at the ferry, but he set the saddle-bags down in the kitchen. There's a fresh cheese and butter and eggs and . . .

Abbess (*seeing the bottle in Heloise's hand*) What's that bottle?

Heloise (*handing it to her*) For you, Mother. From your cousin.

Abbess (*examining the bottle with approval*) We always had a like taste in wine. But it was a risk to send it in this heat. I must have it down to the cellar straight.

Mariella Mother, shall I . . .?

Abbess (*severely, clutching the bottle firmly*) When I need help, I'll ask for it. Presumption is a sin.

Mariella (*meekly*) Yes, Mother.

The Abbess goes out with the wine

In a flash the Nuns cluster excitedly around Heloise. Some of the following dialogue overlaps

(*Kissing Heloise*) Oh, Heloise, it's been so dull without you!

Sister Constance Heloise, how you've grown!

Gisella What kind of a place is Paris?

Sister Laura Is that the way they wear their hair now?

Fifth Nun What's kept you so long? Have you come to stay?

Sister Laura Yes, have you come back to us, child?

Heloise Perhaps. I—I don't know. I . . . (*hemmed in by the Nuns and suddenly nauseated, she sways*)

Sister Constance What is it?

Heloise It's nothing. This place . . . (*she sways, then crumples*)

Mariella She's faint!

The Nuns support Heloise as she falls

Gisella I thought she looked white.

Sister Laura Let her lean on me. Water, Sister.

Gisella fetches a beaker of water

That's right. Don't crowd her, now. Let her breathe. That's better, Here, child.

Heloise (*drinking the water*) It was the heat.

Sister Laura Of course. (*Stroking Heloise's forehead*) The long ride in the hot sun. Lie still, now. Don't try to get up.

Heloise I'm all right. It was only a moment. (*She rises and gives a Nun the beaker*)

Sister Laura Wilful as ever.

Heloise I'm well, really. It's better water here than in Paris. You daren't drink it there. (*Looking round*) Where's Godric?

Mariella (*with a sob in her voice*) Godric . . .
Heloise Where is she?
Sister Constance Didn't you hear?
Mariella She missed the corner step, coming down from the choir.
Gisella You know how dark it is.
Sister Laura And broke her leg.
Heloise Oh no!
Mariella Yes, and it isn't knitting very well.
Sister Laura I'm afraid she's too old.
Fifth Nun Sister Laura is mistress of the novices now. And Reverend
Mother says . . .

The Abbess enters, wiping her lips

Abbess Now, now. That's enough chatter for a while. You can have
Heloise after dinner, before you go to the dorter.
Heloise Mother, may I see Godric?

Nuns and Monks are heard singing in the background

Abbess She's in the infirmary. You know the way.

The lights fade on the Argenteuil Chapel

The Abbess and the Nuns file out.
    *Sister Godric, an old, bent figure, is carried on lying propped up on a litter
bed with a kind of rude reading desk over it. Four Monks bear the litter.
They lay it down, then exit*

Sister Godric lies peering short-sightedly at a book. Heloise approaches her

Godric (*looking up, squinting*) You're not there, I don't believe it, I'm
havin' a vision.

Heloise runs and kneels by her and kisses her

    Holy Mary, but it's herself in person! Well, well.
Heloise Oh my dear—(*Hugging her*)—but you're so thin. Your poor little
wrists—they're no bigger than larks' legs.
Godric (*chuckling*) Larks' legs. That's a good one. I like that. I must make
a mental note. Larks' legs.
Heloise Is it very painful?
Godric Och, the divil can have me legs and welcome, but he's after me eyes
too, the flibbertigibbet. What does it say there, darlin'? (*She pushes her
book at Heloise*)
Heloise (*reading*) "Ah, but they were good days, when you and I sat quiet
among the bookshelves."
Godric So they were, so they were. I must have known you were comin'.
Well now, tell me every mortal t'ing and not a word of lie. Is it a fact that
Master Abelard says you're the best scholar he ever had?
Heloise Where did that come from? My uncle?
Godric Never you mind. Did he say it or didn't he?

Heloise No. But he did say to Gilles de Vannes I was the best *trained* scholar he'd had. And Gilles said he could well believe it, for the teacher who trained me was you.

Godric (*preening herself*) Orgulous as a peacock, that's what I'll be from this day. You've put another ten years on me in Purgatory.

Heloise My first teacher and my dearest friend.

Godric Stop it now or I'll stuff me ears with celery stalks.

Sister Laura comes in

Sister Laura Reverend Mother wants to know if you have the accounts ready, Godric. She's seeing the Steward after Vespers.

Godric (*pulling a face, then speaking firmly*) Tell Reverend Mother the sum for wine for the altar seems excessive, and I'm goin' through it with a toothcomb.

Sister Laura goes out, scared

(*Grinning like a naughty boy*) Drat the things, I clean forgot. Read me those figures, will you, dear, and with God's help I'll do me sums. (*She passes Heloise a parchment*)

Heloise "To cakes for St Martin's. Also wine. Thirty-five sous."

Godric (*writing on another parchment with a quill pen*) "Also wine" is good. Thirty-five.

Heloise "To wine bought before Whitsun. Sixty sous."

Godric Thirty-five and sixty—ninety-five.

Heloise "To wine for the Archdeacon. Twenty-eight sous."

Godric Let's hope he got near enough to smell it. Twenty-eight and ninety-five . . .

Heloise A hundred and twenty-three.

Godric You're right.

Heloise "To twelve pairs of shoes for the poor. Fifteen sous."

Godric Let's see—a hundred and thirty-six?

Heloise Eight.

Godric The Lord sent you. I never could add.

Heloise (*fondly*) Peter can't, either. It's the one thing he's no good at.

Godric (*looking up sharply*) Peter? So it's Peter, is it?

Heloise turns quickly away

Come here a minute. Come.

Reluctantly, Heloise turns to Godric, who peers at her closely

So that's the way of it.

Heloise (*softly, rapt*) To speak his name—to be in the same room—saying nothing, or listening to him talk—it's as if I've been waiting for him from the day I was born. His voice—he has the most wonderful voice—and he knows so much—and tells you things—things that you've always known in your heart and could never find the words to say them. From the first moment I knew, I *knew*. He knew, too, I think. For both of us it was like—coming home.

Godric You frighten me, child.

Heloise Why?

Godric Because you love him so.

Heloise But I *want* to love him. To love and love and give and give—to go on loving and giving—to be *his*—until I die.

Godric Then why have you run away?

Heloise does not answer

Because of the hurt your love could do him?

Heloise (*after a pause; gradually*) It's just begun. I could bear it now—I think I could just bear it—if I never saw him again. But if I go back—if I see him again—then it will be too late to stop—then it will be—for ever. (*She kneels by the litter. Urgently*) Tell me. Tell me!

Godric So that's why you came. For me to say what you want to hear.

Heloise Tell me.

Godric I'll not say it. I'll not make it easy for you.

Heloise Tell me. Like you always did.

Godric Listen, if I've you on me mind as well as meself, me conscience'll be doin' cartwheels. (*She rubs her hands*) Cold out, is it?

Heloise (*rising*) No, it's warm.

Godric When you're old, the sun can boil, you get the shivers. (*Intently*) Ask God. Ask God for guidance.

Heloise I can't. It wouldn't be fair. I only believe in God when I'm desperate.

Godric (*after a moment*) I never could make up me mind whether your infernal honesty was Beelzebub doin' a jig or the latest angel in the makin'.

A bell tolls

There's the bell for Office. You must go to Chapel. Run along now.

Heloise (*kneeling*) Bless me first.

Godric (*placing her hand on Heloise's head*) Holy Mary, Mother of God, bless and keep this loving child, for there's not an ounce of evil in her. Only innocence. (*She crosses herself*)

The bell ceases tolling

Let's hope that's not the lie of the century. Now off with you.

Uncertain, Heloise rises and starts to go

(*Slowly*) My child—

Heloise stops and looks back

—in Donegal, where I come from, they're a superstitious lot. They believe in the unavoidable. There's birth, o' course, and death, o' course, you can't avoid either o' them. But every once in a while, they say, there's somethin' sandwiched 'tween the two—and you can't do nothin' about

that, either. Fate, they call it. Destiny. Oh, they're great on fate in
Donegal. Meself, I don't believe a word of it.

Monks are heard singing in the distance

Send me a sheepskin for the winter. White, if you can. White has the
best wool.

Heloise exits. The lights fade as the Monks carry Godric off.

SCENE 11

Abelard's room in Fulbert's house. Night   **11**

Robert is sitting on a stool. Abelard is standing by the table, holding a whip.

Abelard There. (*Whacking the table with his whip*) A makeshift effort, but
it should serve.
Robert (*tight-lipped*) No.
Abelard Look on it as practice for when you return to Cluny. The scourge
will be expected.
Robert To discipline oneself. Not another.

*Four Monks and six Nuns enter upstage and stand in line, facing across the
stage*

Abelard That's self-indulgence, when another needs it more. (*He thrusts
the whip into Robert's hands*) She may still come back. What do you
think?

Robert does not answer

Have you never loved a woman, Robert?
Robert No, Master.
Abelard Only God?
Robert (*after a pause; at Abelard*) I have never loved a woman.
Abelard (*not missing the distinction, but ignoring it*) Nor I—(*he starts
removing his shirt*)—until now. How old are you?
Robert Twenty-two.
Abelard For the seven years of manhood you have behind you, and the
fifteen before you till you reach my age, I had never loved. I thought
I was incapable of it. And then—suddenly—like an avalanche . . .
(*Naked to the waist, he falls to his knees*) I'm ready.
Robert (*stubbornly*) You're not a priest. You're not subject to the discipline.
Abelard Are only God's ministers allowed to mortify the flesh?
Robert You could fast.
Abelard Yes, and put an edge on every sense I have. What the body lacks,
boy, the mind makes up for. Lord, what an orgy of the mind a fast
induces! No, this is the way—if there is a way.

Reluctantly, Robert starts to scourge Abelard's back

Harder! Harder! Harder!

Robert (*stopping*) No! I can't!

Abelard (*rising and deliberately provoking him*) Her eyes, Robert, her eyes,
her breasts, her young breasts, her mouth—like a balm—her mouth . . .

Robert (*violently*) All right! All right! (*He lashes at Abelard violently re-
peatedly*)   **12**

Abelard cries out. When he has finished, Robert throws down the whip

Abelard (*surprised; painfully*) Well—that was more like it. You know, I
believe you—quite enjoyed it—in the end. Did you—enjoy it, little monk?
In any case—I'm obliged to you. (*Suddenly*) Do you think she went
simply to whet the appetite? No, they say men love to postpone delight,
but women never. Why's that, do you suppose? Eh, boy?

Robert (*trembling*) I—don't know.

Abelard Because men live in their imagination as well as in their senses,
but women only in their senses? Is that it?

Robert I don't know, I tell you, I don't know!

Abelard You must have thought about these things. Not even academically?
You should have, Robert. You're a student. All part of your higher
education. Mind and body, body and mind. A mistake, to nourish the
one and neglect the other. As a virgin of thirty-seven I speak with
authority. Remind me—before term ends—we'll have a symposium on
the subject, shall we? Widen your experience. It should be quite stimulat-
ing. Yes, I can think of one or two of your colleagues, can't you, who are
—how shall I put it?—physically rather less detached . . .?

*Robert falls to his knees and presses his head against Abelard's naked torso.
Abelard strokes the boy's head*

Forgive me. When one is on the rack, there's a vile comfort in seeing a
friend similarly stretched. (*Gently*) Go home now.

Robert Will you sleep?

Abelard No.

Robert (*rising*) I'll sit on the landing.

Abelard No.

Robert I'd like to.

Abelard No! Go home!

Heloise appears quietly in the doorway.
There is a pause, then Robert goes quickly past Heloise and out

Heloise (*eventually*) I was at Argenteuil. They kept me till after Vespers.
Are you angry?

Abelard You're back. Nothing in God's earth or heaven matters. You're
back. (*He collapses at her feet, his whole body shaking, then turns and
looks up at her*)

*Heloise sees the weals across his back. She sinks to her knees beside him.
His arm goes up and enfolds her. The lights fade. Heloise and Abelard exit
in the darkness.*

Gilles' room   **13**

Robert He used to stay and talk when the lecture was over. Hours, he'd
talk, and we'd never know we were hungry. Oh, you don't know how
it was. His lectures, they were like a great wind that leapt suddenly, and
you went with it, the trees tearing and shaking. He was a horse at the
gallop. Now he reads his notes and yawns and is for ever looking at the
hour-glass. They're not afraid of him now. If you heard them snickering
when he comes to the lecture at six, half awake. They've made a song
about it.

> Good argument
> Hath Peter in his head
> But better argument . . .

Gilles I can supply the rhyme.
Robert God knows, we're spirit and flesh. But to see the spirit becoming
flesh before one's eyes . . . (*Tortured*) They make songs about her, too.
Gilles (*fiercely*) You suppose she cares? You think it's the dove and the
hawk? I tell you, boy, you've seen the mating of eagles. And yet—I
know, I know. Never have I seen such madness as this.

Jehan enters with two goblets and a jug of wine

Jehan Master Gilles, will you see Master Alberic of Rheims?
Gilles Why, yes. Come in, Alberic.

Alberic enters, a large and portly figure, very conscious of its dignity

Welcome. Man, even if I hadn't heard it, I'd know from the walk of you
they've made you Master of the Schools at Rheims.

Jehan exits

Gilles shakes Alberic by the hand

Alberic My walk?
Gilles Why not? The spirit should be mirrored in the body. Godliness
makes the face to shine—(*He drops Alberic's hand*)—and the hand to
sweat.

Robert turns as if to go

No, stay, Robert. (*To Alberic*) How long have you been in Paris?
Alberic Since Palm Sunday. I couldn't leave without seeing our Nestorw,
and I have greetings for you from the Archbishop.
Gilles Tell him from me what a distinguished scholastic he's got, if

you've not already done so. Bless me, to think of you sitting in Gerbert's chair.

Alberic I trust the doctrine taught from it will be sounder.

Gilles Safer, anyway. Upon my word, Alberic, at this rate there'll soon be an exodus from Paris to Rheims.

Alberic If the lecture I heard two days ago is a sample of the fare here, the sooner the better.

Robert (*politely*) You were unfortunate sir. Whom did you hear?

Alberic The great Abelard himself. A barren wit. I always knew it. Would you believe it, the lecture I heard on Monday was, with one exception, the same I heard him give three years ago, at Laon?

Gilles A marvellous memory, yours, Alberic. It must be the secret of your success.

Alberic My memory is tolerably good. But I have special reason to recall this lecture. It was the first he had the gall to give—without a licence.

Gilles I understood he was challenged to it. Is that so?

Alberic In a manner, yes. He had the impudence to declare that in theology a man needs no master save Holy Writ and his own intelligence.

Gilles A dangerous doctrine. Accept it and half of us would be out of a job. And so you challenged it?

Alberic I did.

Gilles And he lectured, I suppose, to empty benches?

Alberic There are always lovers of novelty. He drew the lighter sort.

Gilles A handful of irresponsibles.

Alberic Exactly.

Gilles Robert, wine for Master Alberic.

Robert pours wine into the two goblets for Gilles and Alberic

Robert is on leave from Cluny to study at Notre-Dame.

Alberic Oh? Under whom?

Robert Under the greatest master in Christendom. Master Peter Abelard.

Alberic (*flushing*) What did you say?

Gilles Now, now, Alberic. Mayn't a student be loyal to his master?

Alberic Loyal! To a master who can't master himself?

Robert goes to drag Alberic to his feet

A man who's a wencher, a lecher and a . . .

Gilles (*thundering*) Robert!!

Robert, about to strike Alberic across the face, lowers his arm

Alberic I suppose you know, if they teach you any canon law at Cluny, that would have meant excommunication?

Robert You know nothing about him. He was never your master.

Robert turns and goes quickly out

Alberic (*grimly*) What dunghill was that cockerel reared on?

Gilles (*pouring wine*) His father is Squire of Montboissier.

Alberic (*shaken*) What?

Gilles (*blandly*) And if I'm not mistaken you'll some day be telling in your cups how you once threatened excommunication to the Abbot of Cluny.

Alberic That one Abbot of Cluny?

Gilles As soon, I think, as his years allow.

Alberic He'd best first learn to mind his temper.

Gilles Even when provoked, I agree. Come, you did spit at Abelard. I don't quite know why.

Alberic If you don't, you're the only man in Paris who doesn't—except, I'm told, the old fool, her uncle. I tried to hint something of it to him today.

Gilles Abelard is consumed with love . . .

Alberic Love? The sexuality of the sewer. Insatiable concupiscence. I tell you, Gilles, that man's the most depraved it's ever been my misfortune to . . .

Abelard, with a book, enters

Abelard It's not, is it? Yes, it is. Old Alberic! Well done, man. Rheims has got a good mastiff.

Alberic You'll excuse me, Gilles. I have to sup with the Bishop.

Gilles Where else? Alberic attended your lecture on Monday, Peter.

Abelard Really? Morning or afternoon?

Alberic There was no morning lecture. It was cancelled.

Abelard So it was, so it was. You must have heard me on the Trinity.

Alberic For the second time. One addition surprised me.

Abelard Only one?

Alberic I noted that, whilst you grant that God begat God you deny that God begat himself.

Abelard That is so. If you wish, I'll be happy to explain the reason.

Alberic I am not concerned with reason. I ask only for the word of authority.

Abelard You shall have it.

Abelard "Whoso attributes to God the power of begetting himself is the more in error because it is not so, not only in respect of God, but of all creatures, corporal or spiritual: for there is nothing whatever that begets itself." St Augustine. Book One. Chapter One.

Alberic Yes, yes, of course, but it must be rightly interpreted.

Abelard I heartily agree. But what you asked for was the word of authority, not its meaning. However, if you have a moment, I'll be pleased to explain how you've fallen into heresy.

Alberic Heresy?

Abelard (*affably*) The heresy which declares that the Father is his own Son.

Speechless, Alberic storms out. Abelard replaces the book

Gilles Peter, Peter. Another enemy.

Abelard Well, I've no use for these dialectical bully-boys. And Alberic—God, what a bladder of lard! What a hill of suet!

Jehan enters

Jehan Your supper, Master?
Gilles Will you stay and eat it with me, Peter?
Abelard No, I—I have to get back.

Jehan goes

There is a sudden constraint between Gilles and Abelard. Gilles drinks. Eventually Abelard holds out the book he has brought in

She asked me to return this.
Gilles My Homer. She could have brought it herself. I wouldn't have snapped. Is she well?

Abelard nods

And you? Then, good-night, Peter.
Abelard (*initimately*) Gilles—it's indescribable. As if we'd—invented a new emotion.
Gilles Don't all lovers feel that?
Abelard She's captured my life. I'm—helpless—before a girl of seventeen.
Gilles Even if it were Trojan Helen—Cleopatra—Aphrodite—even then it would be madness.
Abelard But it's not. It's Heloise . . .
Gilles I've not knelt to God for fifteen years. I would pray for you—if I could. For both of you.
Abelard All the faith in France can't stop it now.

Abelard goes quickly. There is a pause

Gilles takes the cushion from his chair, throws it on the ground, and lowers himself painfully to his knees

Gilles "O Lamb of God that takest away the sins of the world, have mercy upon us. O Lamb of God that takest away the sins of the world, have mercy upon us—

Jehan enters with a plate of fish

—O Lamb of God that takest away the sins of the world, receive our prayer."

The "Agnus Dei" is heard. Jehan stops in disbelief. The lights fade

Jehan and Gilles exit in the darkness

Scene 13

Abelard's room in Fulbert's house   **14**

The room is lit by a faint blur of moonlight

The Nuns enter and face downstage. The Monks enter and kneel at their feet, facing upstage. Heloise enters, naked, from one side. Abelard enters, naked, from the other

Heloise Hold me—hold me, Peter—closer—closer still.

There is a long, deep embrace. She sighs happily

   Now I'm safe.

He looks down at her, strokes her hair, chuckles

   Why do you laugh?
Abelard There's a warning. About women. Proverbs. Chapter Four.
Heloise Verse Ten.

The Nuns lift their heads and raise their hands slowly so that the movements are completed by the word "Darling" below, when they all sigh, lower their heads to look at the Monks and lower their hands to cup round the Monks' faces

   "Let thy heart not be drawn into the ways of woman." (*Slowly sinking to her knees*) "Lose not thyself in her paths. For her house is the way to hell. She is the net of the hunter. Her heart is a snare. Her hands are chains. He who pleaseth God escapes her, but the sinner is her prey."
Abelard You know it?
Heloise I had to learn it once as a punishment.
Abelard (*kneeling to face her*) Am I your prey, my darling?
Heloise I hope so, Oh, I hope so, Peter. (*Sinking to lie back on the floor*) Love me. Love me.

Abelard goes down on the floor beside her. There is the sound of a walking-stick scraping against a door in the tower. The Monks rise

Abelard What's that?
Heloise (*in a whisper*) Guibert. He's always late to bed.
Abelard He must be drunk.

They return to their embrace

   Someone fumbles with the latch of the door. It opens. Fulbert stands there, fully dressed. The Monks swing round to watch with accusing faces

Fulbert (*looking down at them*) They told me, and I loathed them. I loathed them for lying.

Heloise reaches for a fur rug and wraps it round her

   It's all right—it's a lie—it's a lie—(*Screaming*)—it's a lie! (*He raises his stick to strike Abelard, then sways and falls to the ground, the stick crashing with him*)

Abelard catches him as he falls. Fulbert lies breathing stertorously, his mouth awry

Abelard Quick, the light. I think it's a stroke.
Heloise I'll get Yvonne. (*She moves away*)

Abelard lays Fulbert gently back on the floor. Heloise returns

Peter, I've just remembered. Yvonne—she's out.
Abelard At this hour? Where?
Heloise The Watchnight Service. Peter, it's Good Friday.

The lights fade to Black-out. All the bells of Notre-Dame peal out a triumphant diapason.

SCENE 14

A narrow cloister of the Cathedral. It is the morning of Easter Day **15**

Proceeding to the Cathedral, Bernard, Abbot of Clairvaux, austere and austerely garbed, enters, followed by Gilles de Vannes, in full Canonicals. The sound of the bells continues, muted

Gilles I tell you, Bernard, the thing is impossible.
Bernard With God all things are possible.
Gilles Amen. But, by your leave. Bernard, you and he are not yet identical.

Bernard smiles

Thank God you can still laugh at yourself. Smile like that at young Robert de Montboissier and he might just go back to Clairvaux with you.
Bernard If a man has once seen the face of God, as Robert did, and then turns from it, it were better for him he had never been born, for he has crucified the Son of God afresh.
Gilles Bernard, Robert did not turn from God's face but from your face. And if this were not Easter morning I should tell you that in leaving Clairvaux, where the brethren kneel in green slime on the chapel floor, for Cluny, where his bed if hard was at least dry, he crucified not the Son of God but your pride.

The bells fade out

Bernard My pride? Is it possible any man on this earth should think me proud?
Gilles There's only one man prouder than Bernard of Clairvaux and that is Peter Abelard.
Bernard Abelard!
Gilles And now you'll be using the discipline on those thin shoulders for weeks, for fear I may be right.
Bernard (*humbly*) God knows you may be.

Heloise, radiant in blue cloak and hood, enters behind them and starts to cross the stage. Looking eagerly about her as she passes, she pauses at Bernard's side

Heloise Forgive me, Father.

Bernard steps back

(*Crossing below Gilles*) Gilles!

Heloise goes

Bernard Who was that?
Gilles A friend. We share an interest in Homer.
Bernard A friend. Of course. I have never seen a face that had so markedly
the makings of a saint.
Gilles Quite. Her name is Heloise.
Bernard (*rigid*) Not Abelard's whore?
Gilles She would, I think, so describe herself.
Bernard God bless my soul!
Gilles He will, Bernard, never doubt it.

*Figures start to enter Notre Dame, Monks, with surplices over their habits,
carrying candelabra and one single pole candle, Nuns wearing candle head-
dresses and carrying candles. They take up positions in the background*

Bernard That one can look as she looks, and her soul be mired with the
filthiest sin of the flesh! Truly, God's ways are past understanding.
Gilles (*placidly*) You amaze me, Bernard. I always thought you had the key
to them. Shall we go in?

*Bernard and Gilles go into the Cathedral
Heloise enters, followed by Abelard, who wears his master's gown and
doctor's hood over his finest tunic*

Abelard (*distraught*) Why didn't you tell me sooner? Why?
Heloise I was going to on Friday night, and then . . .
Abelard It may not be so. You may be mistaken.
Heloise No. I'm quite certain. I've been reading Aristotle to find out.
Abelard Reading Aristotle. Dear God, and I've brought you to this.
Heloise But I'm *glad*, Peter, can't you see? I've never been so happy.
Especially now that you've left my uncle's house—(*she puts Abelard's
hand to her stomach*)—because now I have something of you with me
always. The richest thing I ever had.
Abelard Oh, my dear love. (*With decision*) One thing's certain. You can't
stay in Paris. I shall take you home.
Heloise Home?
Abelard To Le Palais. To my sister.
Heloise I can't leave my uncle yet.
Abelard When?
Heloise Master Simon says he should be up in a week.
Abelard Very well. In a week. But first—we must marry.
Heloise (*instantly*) No!

Abelard Heloise . . .

Heloise No, that is one sin I will not commit! You know what they call me? Abelard's whore.

Abelard Abelard's whore!

Heloise I glory in it. I wear it like a crown, Peter.

Abelard You'll marry me and be my wife.

Heloise Not wife—but so much more than wife.

Abelard My wife. My wife before the world!

Heloise No! The priests write history. Would you have them say of me that Heloise made Abelard a nobody?

Abelard History! I'm concerned with *now*.

Heloise I won't ruin you, Peter.

Abelard You speak as if marriage were adultery.

Heloise It is a kind of adultery, for you. Remember Evrard?

Abelard Evrard was a priest. He'd taken vows. I'm not ordained.

Heloise You've gone half-way to God. You belong to the Civitas Dei. In the eyes of the world you're sworn to continence.

Three Monks enter the cathedral with ornate robes over habits and surplices. The centre Monk wears a bishop's head-dress and robe, and carries a crozier. In front of and behind him are the Crucifers carrying golden crosses. They move to the altar, then stand behind it, the Bishop slightly above the Crucifers, who raise their crosses high

Abelard Don't you want our son to have a name?

Heloise Not if in giving it to him I destroy his father's.

Abelard (*after a pause*) You don't love me enough.

Heloise Oh, Peter, Peter, I will love you with all my soul to the last moment of my dying breath. But marry me and you won't just be breaking faith with your future, you'll be breaking faith with something you pledged yourself to before you were tonsured.

Abelard I break faith every time I take you in my arms.

Heloise I know you do. I know we're living in what the Church calls fornication, even if it's burnt up Heaven and Earth into such a glory that I cry out in adoration of it when I should be on my knees repenting it. But I've accepted that. I know it's a sin. Don't ask me to sprinkle it with holy water.

Abelard But your reputation—your good name . . .

Heloise Oh, my darling, don't you know I'd fling the world away and heaven with it to have you love me for an afternoon? Without you, nothing. With you, all things. What else matters in the Universe?

Abelard I could lay my head in the dust.

Heloise I'd lie there with you, like your shadow. Be happy, Peter. I am. Wildly happy. And in seven days I'll go with you to Le Palais.

Abelard You swear it?

Heloise Where else should our son be born, but in his father's house? **16**

Abelard takes Heloise in his arms, and they are lost to all but each other.

As they embrace, the Cathedral blazes with light and echoes with the sound of "Gloria Patri" from the Victoria Magnificat. The candelabras overhead and candles on and around the altar flicker as they burn. The Nuns switch on their candle head-dresses and candlesticks. The Monks switch on their candles and candelabras. The Bishop and Crucifers turn upstage and, led by the Bishop, move in procession to the altar.

As the Choral Eucharist reaches its climax, Heloise breaks from Abelard's embrace and exits

Abelard turns and stares transfixed at the Cross. The Cathedral lights fade and a light comes up on Abelard

Abelard (*turning downstage*) O God, who didst fashion me of earth, how can I but smell of it!
Congregation (*in a shout*) AMEN! AMEN! AMEN!

The lights Black-out

CURTAIN

ACT II

SCENE 1

Outside the homestead at Le Palais, Brittany. Spring, a year later

Dappled lighting comes up on an apple orchard. Abelard is stretched out on a grass bank in the sun. Denise, his sister, a placid countrywoman, sits on a bench peeling mushrooms. In one corner is a wooden cradle. Two monks stand on an upper level of one tower, holding gilded branches. Distant music is heard from a pipe, and a bird song

Abelard Peaceful.

Denise Mm?

Abelard Still and peaceful. Everything.

Denise It's Sunday.

Abelard So it is (*He stretches*) With all the saints intent on the prayers of the faithful and the whole world droning with devotion like a hive of bees. (*He toys with a bloom in his hand*) I wonder what Adam thought, his first spring outside Paradise, when the thorns that had cursed him all winter broke into anything so small and white and tender as this. (*He sits up*)

The pipe and bird song fade out

The springs I've wasted inside towns. To think that I could have lived and died here, ploughed and sown, had half a dozen like young Peter. (*He rises and goes to the cradle*) I envy you, Denise.

Denise You've written books. I've had children. Each is a way of life.

Abelard Yes, but mine . . . (*Suddenly*) He's not breathing.

Denise You don't say.

Abelard I tell you, my son's chest is not moving, I can hear no sound. (*He prods the baby*)

Denise They don't roar like a hurricane at four months—

The child starts to yell

—unless, of course, some fool of a father prods them in the belly.

Abelard I was just testing—making sure . . .

Heloise comes quickly out of the house, goes to the cradle, rocks it, and dandles a sprig of blossom in the child's face

Is—he quite fit? Not—sick, is he?

The baby stops crying. Heloise exchanges glances with Denise, who rolls her eyes at the idiocy of men. Heloise smiles at Abelard and murmurs endearments at the baby

(*To Denise*) Is it some sort of mirage of the heart or is she *really* lovelier than ever?

Denise It suits her here—and when you're able to be with her—must you go back tomorrow?

Hugh, Denise's husband, comes through the orchard carrying a wooden pail, and moves to the pump. Children's voices from inside the house call "Mama, Mama"

Hugh There's the children back from catechism.
Children (*off*) Mama!
Denise Yes, all right, I'm coming.

Denise goes, unhurried, into the house

Hugh (*pumping water into the pail*) I was thinking —we might have a bit of fishing, if you could stay.
Abelard I'm sorry, Hugh, I'd have liked to fish with you.

Heloise looks around, something on her mind. Eventually:

Hugh Queer, how Lent and the close season for trout overlap.

Hugh goes into the house

Heloise Your last day. (*She comes to Abelard*)
Abelard (*putting an arm lightly round her*) How *tenderly* I love you now.
Heloise When will you come again?
Abelard Make it unnecessary. Come back with me to Paris. Be my wife.

Heloise at once moves away out of his arm

It's God's way, Heloise.
Heloise For the layman, not the cleric.
Abelard Now listen—will you listen to me?
Heloise Not the cleric, Peter.
Abelard Will you . . .?
Heloise No. I'll listen to Terence, Jerome, Cicero, Josephus, Pythagoras, Socrates . . .
Abelard Yes, yes, yes, you've quoted the classics on the subject till I'm dizzy. God knows who taught you such scholarship.
Heloise You did.
Abelard A grave mistake. Women should be kept illiterate. Oh, my darling, what are you afraid of?
Heloise Losing you.
Abelard And to marry me would be to part for ever? A curious logic, even for a woman.
Heloise I'm not ashamed to be called your harlot. I would be ashamed to be called your wife.
Abelard I beg you . . .
Heloise No. I'll do no harm as your harlot. They'll only laugh and sing a song about it, and with me away in Brittany, they'll forget. My darling, it's death in life each time you go away, but you'll come back and we shall still be happy.

Abelard (*after a pause*) How God looks upon us I can't tell. When all the good that's in me is bound up with loving you, how can it be evil? But it may be so—and if it is there's penance for it.

Heloise Then do penance and be absolved.

Abelard There's something else. (*Painfully*) The old man trusted me. I ate at his table, slept under his roof, shared his home. He trusted me—and I betrayed his trust. Don't you see? It's not just between you and me, or us and God, it's between me and him. A point of honour.

Heloise (*with a burst of bitterness, almost hysteria*) Honour! A point of honour! Oh, a man and his honour! How can a woman ever answer *that*?

Abelard What answer is there? What can you set against it?

Heloise Instinct.

Abelard An abstraction.

Heloise Honour, instinct. Two abstractions. Or is honour a concrete thing?

Abelard I was brought up to believe that it was.

Heloise These masculine codes—they have no meaning to a woman, Peter!

Abelard Then do it because I ask it.

Heloise Knowing it's wrong?

Abelard If necessary, yes.

Heloise Ah, that's not fair . . .

Abelard Do it for *me*, Heloise.

Heloise (*torn*) Peter, you don't know the power you have over people . . .

Abelard Do it for me.

Heloise I—I've never refused you anything—oh, God . . .

Abelard For *me*, Heloise. For *me*.

Heloise It's wrong, Peter, I know, I know it's wrong!

Abelard (*eagerly*) But you'll do it? Yes? Heloise?

Heloise I can only say—the grief that's to come will be no less than the love that went before it. (*Helplessly*) Yes! Yes, I'll do it!

Overjoyed, he sweeps her off her feet, and whirls her round in his arms

Abelard Denise! Denise! Here! Quickly!

Heloise Put me down!

Abelard Why? (*Putting her down*) You're not pregnant again, are you?

Heloise Of course not, but . . .

Hugh enters

Hugh You'd best look at the mare if you're going to ride her tomorrow, Peter. I think she's lame.

Denise hurries out of the house

Denise What is it? What's wrong?

Abelard Nothing. Hugh says the mare's lame. Oh, and we're going to be married.

Abelard goes with Hugh

Denise (*embracing Heloise*) Oh, my dear. Ever since that first night when I saw Hugh lift you down from your horse, it's what I've prayed for.

Heloise And I have prayed against.

Denise Against?

Heloise It's the end of any great place for him in the Church.

Denise I never could see Peter a bishop.

Heloise They could take the Schools from him.

Denise Wherever Peter is, the Schools will be. He emptied Paris once. If they turn him out, he'll do it again.

Heloise Don't *you* think he's wrong to marry?

Denise I think he'd be wrong not to. Oh, I went with Hugh a whole summer before we were married and wasn't ashamed, at least not in my heart. And yet, once I'd married him—it's like drinking when you're thirsty. You feel better if you stop to say a Benedicat over it.

Heloise A ritual of pretty words. What difference does that make?

Denise The difference is that I could say my prayers before I went to bed with him. I couldn't before. It seemed like cheating.

Heloise (*thoughtfully*) I don't say any prayers, except for Peter. So it doesn't matter.

Abelard enters briskly

Abelard Well, do we have your blessing?

Denise (*kissing him*) Where will it be? Here?

Abelard No, Paris. (*To Heloise*) We'll need your uncle's consent.

Denise In view of the child, could he refuse?

Abelard I don't see how he can. Now, we'd better not ride in publicly, side by side. It might look as if we're defying convention just when we're bowing to it. We'll have to get you into the city by stealth. The question is how.

Denise I know how.

Denise hurries into the house

Heloise Peter, the marriage must be a secret.

Abelard Of course. Until we get home. And then all Paris shall know that Abelard and Heloise are man and wife.

Heloise (*urgently*) No one must know, except my uncle. Promise me—no one.

Abelard Not even the priest?

Heloise smiles

Denise enters with a voluminous black garment over her arm

Denise (*to Heloise*) Here. Slip this on over your dress.

Heloise (*drawing back instinctively*) What is it?

Denise Only a nun's habit. (*To Abelard*) It was Mother's. Remember?

Reluctantly Heloise allows the creased black draperies to be lowered over her head. Suddenly she screams. Abelard goes to her

Heloise No! I can't! I can't! Peter! (*She struggles with the folds, becoming hopelessly entangled*)

Abelard tears the robe off her. She stands shaking with fright

Abelard What is it?

Heloise I don't know. I—I suppose it was what Godric meant when she used to say that she could feel someone walking over her grave . . .

Heloise stands trembling as the lights fade to a Black-out. A single bell **17** *tolls*

Scene 2

The narrow cloister of Notre-Dame

Echoing voices, rising and falling, are heard calling "Fulbert—Fulbert— Fulbert—Fulbert". Five Nuns enter and form with the Monks two oblique lines between the towers, Fulbert enters; he is older and shabbier, and moves slowly, leaning on his stick. Abelard enters to him. He is cloaked. The echoing voices die away

Abelard Fulbert! I *will* speak with you.

Fulbert You—you dare to—in the very precincts of the Cathedral . . .

Abelard Three times I've been to the house . . .

Fulbert And three times I have said I will not see you! Yes, and I'll say it three hundred times if . . .

Abelard Quiet, man. Listen.

The Monks and Nuns turn to look at Abelard

Fulbert There is nothing to be said between us. Nothing!

Abelard Very well. Then I shall take her back to Brittany.

Fulbert *Back?* You mean she's here? Here in Paris?

Abelard Yes, with the child.

Fulbert A child!

Abelard A fine boy. Four months.

Fulbert So—there's a child.

Abelard I came to tell you—and to ask you for her hand in marriage.

Fulbert (*thunderstruck*) You—would *marry*?

Abelard There's a condition.

Fulbert Ah, conditions, conditions. I don't like conditions.

Abelard I don't like them either. The condition is hers, not mine. The marriage must be secret.

Fulbert A secret marriage? No!

Abelard If I had my way I'd shout it from the roofs of Paris, but she'll have it a secret or nothing.

Fulbert No!

Abelard Listen, and carefully. Afterwards, if you agree, she'll come back and live with you again, just as she used to. We'll live apart—provided we may see each other whenever we wish. Well?

There is a pause

Heloise, cloaked, enters and sits downstage

Fulbert I must think. I don't like secrets, don't like secrets, no. I must weigh the position. Balance the possibilities. Yes, indeed—I must think. (*He starts towards the Cathedral*)

Abelard Fulbert, don't you want to see her?

The Monks and Nuns turn away

Fulbert (*turning back*) See her? See her? No, I won't see her—I won't see anyone . . .

A spotlight comes up on Heloise. Fulbert stares

Heloise Uncle . . .

Fulbert (*at length*) My little dove—my darling. (*He looks at Heloise pathetically*) Does life break every man? In wrath remember mercy. I must—I must think . . .

The lights fade

The Nuns exit. The Monks form another group, watching the ensuing **18** *scene*

SCENE 3

The crypt of St Aignan's Chapel. A chill dawn.

Gilles stands at a small, makeshift altar. Abelard and Heloise are kneeling side by side. Fulbert stands behind them. There are sounds of a tinker riding by calling his wares, jangling pots, a dog barking

Gilles (*reading hurriedly*) Benedic, Domine, hunc anullum, quem nos in tuo nomine benedicimus, ut quae eum gestaverit, fidelitatem integram suo sponso tenens, in pace et voluntate tua permaneat, atque in mutua caritate semper vivat. Per Christum Dominum Nostrum.

Fulbert's eyes never leave Abelard and Heloise

Heloise }
Abelard } Amen.

Gilles (*perfunctorily*) Repeat after me.

Abelard repeats each sentence

With this ring I thee wed; this gold and silver I thee give; with my body I
thee worship; and with all my worldly goods I thee endow.

Abelard places the ring on Heloise's thumb

In the name of the Father—

Abelard transfers the ring to her second finger

—and of the Son

Abelard transfers the ring to her third finger

—and of the Holy Ghost.

Abelard transfers the ring to her fourth finger and leaves it there

Amen. Confirma hoc, Deus, quod operatus est in nobis. A templo sancto
tuo, quod est in Jerusalem. (*He turns away and closes the book*)

Abelard Kyrie eleison.
Heloise Christe eleison.
Abelard Kyrie eleison.

*Abelard and Heloise cross themselves. Heloise is strained and shivering.
Abelard kisses her tenderly. She forces a smile. Gilles puts on his fur cape*

Heloise It's cold. (*She rises*)

Fulbert gestures at Heloise with his stick

Heloise exits, and Fulbert follows

*Abelard instinctively makes to follow also, but Fulbert, as he goes, bars the
way with his stick*

Abelard Well, it's done. (*He pulls his cloak about him*)
Gilles More's the pity. Abelard married—there'll be fine songs about that.
Abelard There'll be no songs.
Gilles Ha!
Abelard I have his word.
Gilles *His* word! That's a strong tower. Did you see his eyes, man? Like
the flash of an adder in the long grass.
Abelard No, no, no. He swore by St Michael and all the Angels.
Gilles They say Providence has a care for children and fools. I've small use
for either. (*He picks up his book and cloth and moves away*)
Abelard Won't you wish me well?
Gilles (*deeply troubled*) I believe it would be better to wish you a broken
neck.
Abelard Better a broken neck than broken faith.
Gilles And that from the master of logic, that from the voice of reason, that
from the mind that set the century ablaze! You've had too much trade
with words, Peter. (*Bitterly*) But there—no matter. Some day—it may be
a hundred years from now—it may be two hundred—but some day
another will speak of reason as you once did, and bring together the whole

summa of theology by just such methods as yours—and they will write *his* name in the Calendar of Saints and handle *his* work as if it were the Ark of the Covenant. And where will Abelard be? Smashed. Forgotten. A deserter from that little band of immortals who alone give a measure of meaning to man's existence. And for what? A woman. You fool, Peter. You—no, not fool—clown. You naïve and total clown. (*He moves away again*)

Abelard Gilles—thank you for making her my wife.

Gilles Whom the gods would destroy they first make sentimental.

Gilles goes

Abelard looks about him

Abelard It shouldn't be like this. All the bells should ring for us.

Silence. The lights fade. Abelard exits in the darkness

SCENE 4   **19**

Abelard's old room and the landing off it. Night

There is a table with books, and a chair

Heloise hurries in. She is cloaked

Heloise (*urgently*) Peter.

> *Robert enters with a book. The Monks move away and are joined by two others and by Nuns, who place themselves by the towers and peer through with hard, accusing faces*

Oh!

Robert He said I could—he offered me the use of his books while he's away.

Heloise Away?

Robert At Liége. The convocation.

Heloise (*momentarily stunned, then sinking down exhausted*) I forgot. He won't be back till Friday.

Robert Friday noon.

Heloise Oh, God, where are you leading us?

Robert You're hurt.

Heloise No. Just—tired.

Robert Your cheek's bruised and swollen—and your arm's bleeding.

Heloise It's nothing. I—I fell.

Robert There's a contusion. I'll get some water.

Heloise No, no—thank you, but I must be out of Paris before it's light.

Robert (*getting a bowl of water, a shirt and a bandage*) You'd better let me. You can't go like that. You'll have everyone staring and pointing.

Heloise I'm used to it.

Robert Pull your sleeve back.

Heloise It's nothing, I tell you.

Robert Do as I say. (*He bathes her cheek*)

Heloise (*after a silence*) Why are you doing this for me?

Silence

> Robert?

Robert Not for you.

Heloise (*after a pause*) It wasn't a fall.

Robert You don't have to say anything.

Heloise You're Peter's friend. He trusts you. Master Alberic came to the house.

Robert Yes?

Heloise Alberic of Rheims. I'd never seen him before.

Robert Fat and small eyes peeping. (*He dabs at her wrist*)

Heloise That's right. He told my uncle he'd always wanted to see his books, but he didn't come for that—he came to spy. (*She winces*)

Robert Sorry.

Heloise Geoffrey of Chartres was there too—just back from Rome.

Robert (*starting to bandage the wrist*) Nice man.

Heloise Very. He said something about having more consequence in Rome as Peter Abelard's friend than as the Bishop-Elect of Chartres, and my uncle said that made him proud as he'd always thought of me as a daughter and to know I was married to so great a man . . .

Robert stops bandaging and stares

> Yes. A month ago. Oh, I denied it, of course. I said I was his mistress. My uncle struck me. He—he clawed at me. They pulled him away, but Alberic had got what he came for. It'll be all over Paris by morning, Do you still want to help me now?

There is a silence. Robert picks up the bowl, shirt, etc., and puts them on the table

> It's not safe any more in my uncle's house. Not safe in Paris. Will you tell Peter I've gone to Argenteuil, to Sister Godric, with the little boy?

Robert I'll tell him. Go now, please.

Heloise I don't know how to thank you . . .

Robert (*violently*) Don't! Just go!

Heloise (*after a pause*) You love him too, don't you, very much? Oh, not as I love him, but . . .

Robert (*savagely*) Exactly as you love him. Exactly.

Heloise looks at him with compassion

> Yes.

Heloise goes, watched by the Nuns and Monks

The lights fade to a Black-out. Robert exits in the darkness with the bowl and bandages. Nuns are heard singing "Deus in Adjutorium"

SCENE 5

Argenteuil   **20**

A pool of light reveals the sitting Nuns grouped in a semi-circle round the Abbess, among them Heloise, in a dark dress

Abbess Holy Silvester—
Sister Constance Intercede for her soul.
Abbess Holy Gregory—
Sister Laura Intercede for her soul.
Abbess Holy Martin—
Mariella Intercede for her soul.
Abbess Holy Alexis—
Gisella Intercede for her soul.
Abbess Holy Magdalene—
A Nun Intercede for her soul.
Abbess Holy Felicitas—
A Nun Intercede for her soul.
Abbess (*in her deepest tones*) Go forth, Christian and holy Spirit, from this world. Go in peace: in the name of angels and archangels: in the name of principalities and powers and all the strength of heaven: in the name of Cherubim and Seraphim: in the name of the whole human race which is written in the Book of Life. Let the angels come to meet thee on thy way and bring thee into the City. Lord Jesus Christ, receive the soul of thy servant Godric.
Nuns Amen.

The Abbess crosses herself

Abbess Four of you will go to the chapel and take the place of those now keeping watch. The rest of you will go to the dorter and lie down on your beds, and let there be no reading or talking, for you had little enough sleep last night. No one is to rise till the bell rings for Nones, and perhaps we shall have less of that slovenly singing in the choir, such as this morning. The four for the vigil until Nones will be Gisella, Audere, Constance— Heloise, Godric was your friend, let you be the fourth. Ave Maria purissima.
Nuns Conceived without sin.

The Nuns and Heloise go out

The Abbess goes to the table on which is a vessel of Communion wine and a goblet. She pours wine into the goblet and drinks

Mariella comes flying in

Mariella Reverend Mother! Reverend Mother!
Abbess Mariella!

Mariella stops in her tracks

(*Scowling and wiping her lips*) *When* may we run, Mariella?
Mariella To—assist at a deathbed or from a fire, Reverend Mother.
Abbess Is yet another of our community in extremis?
Mariella No, Reverend Mother.
Abbess Are we on fire, child?
Mariella I—it's not—there's a man . . .

Abelard strides in

Mariella kneels, frightened, crossing herself

Abelard (*desperately*) Who is it? Who is it who's died here? In God's
name!
Abbess One of our sisters. Godric. May her soul be blessed.
Abelard Godric—Godric . . . (*At length, controlling himself*). Forgive
me. I rode through the village. They said there'd been a death up at the
Convent. No one knew who it—Godric. I'm sorry. She was her friend.
Abbess Mariella, go to the chapel and call Heloise. You will take her place.
Mariella At once, Mother.

Mariella starts to run, remembers, slows to a walk, and exits

Abbess(*pouring wine into the goblet*) Sit down a moment and calm yourself,
Master Peter.
Abelard You know me?
Abbess Taking the veil does not necessarily make one half-witted. (*She
hands Abelard the goblet*)
Abelard Thank you, no, I . . .
Abbess Drink it, man. You look like a sepulchre.

Abelard drinks obediently

Heloise enters

(*To Heloise*) Remember. This is your home for as long as you need us.

The Abbess returns the goblet to the table and goes out

Abelard stands, drinking Heloise in

Abelard I thought it was you who was dead.
Heloise My darling . . .

There is a great distance between them

Abelard All last night—I was half asleep in the saddle—I seemed to keep finding you and losing you. I was wandering on strange roads, standing in strange houses, watching for you to come to me. And when I got here —I'd have seen the whole convent dead of the plague if it meant that you'd come through that door alive. God, it's quiet. Like the stillness before the Last Day. Is it always like this?

Heloise More so today, perhaps. Last night everyone had to get up to see Godric die. They're dead with sleep.

Abelard Is there nowhere else we can talk?

Heloise One of the novices is to be received tomorrow. Her people are in the guest-house.

Abelard The garden?

Heloise It's beyond the graveyard. The sexton is digging Godric's grave.

Abelard Come here—at least let me feel you near me.

Heloise I daren't be near you, Peter. I—I daren't.

Deeply physically aware, they try to keep apart

Abelard I was away when you needed me. He struck you.

Heloise It's not myself I'm afraid for. It's you. Peter, don't go back to Paris.

Abelard My dear girl, what possible harm could he do me?

Heloise I don't know. I think he's mad. Peter, don't go back.

Abelard You know I must.

Heloise Yes, you must. (*After a pause; to herself*) Now it begins. "Oh, they're great on fate in Donegal."

Abelard What?

Heloise Peter, I've been thinking. I must stay here now for a while. I shall ask Reverend Mother if I can wear novice's dress. No, please, my darling, listen. We'll let it be known that in a year or two I shall take the veil.

Abelard Heloise, are you utterly . . .

Heloise Dear sweet Peter, can you *see* me as a nun? But if we can make people believe it, the talk will die. Because the marriage would be annulled, wouldn't it, if I joined the Sisterhood? My darling, you're looking at me as though I were a ghost. It's only a tale to give the lie to my uncle. As if any vows on earth could keep me from you!

Without thinking, she is in his arms

Abelard (*holding her in a vice*) Swear you'll never—not even a novice— not even a lay sister . . .

Heloise You're hurting!

Abelard Swear!

Heloise I've no vocation, they wouldn't receive me, even if I . . .

Abelard (*violently*) Swear it!

Heloise All right, I swear, I swear, I swear!

Desperate, reckless, consumed with an intangible fear, he crushes her to him, feels for her breast

No, Peter—no, not here—(*crying out*) oh, God—not here . . .

But her head falls back, her body bends with his and her eyes go blind
The lights fade to Black-out

Abelard and Heloise exit in the darkness

SCENE 6

A Paris street. Late evening. Shadows everywhere   **21**

Guibert, Alain, Gerard, Philippe and Jehan enter singing or humming "When
Summer On is Stealing". Fulbert enters and watches the ensuing scene, leaning
heavily on his stick. Alys and a Young Whore enter and stroll invitingly. Guibert,
eager, moves towards Alys, but Alain and Gerard move across his path and take
Alys to the tower, into which she climbs. Guibert stands dejected. Another
Student enters, exchanges words with Alain and Gerard, and follows Alys up
the stairs. Alain and Gerard exit. Two heavily cloaked and hooded figures
enter, Meanwhile the Young Whore, seizing her chance, moves hopefully
towards Guibert, but he rejects her and turns away, feeling his empty purse.
The Young Whore, the Students, Jehan and Philippe sit or recline at the back
of the stage. Fulbert moves slowly to Guibert

Fulbert That song, Guibert—about the summer coming in and a young
  wench—you used to sing it when you were here. If I remember rightly, it
  was one of Master Peter's. (*He offers him a coin*)
Guibert (*taking the money*) I—I believe so, your Reverence.
Fulbert They tell me it's still very popular.
Guibert Well—it's a love song. We all like songs about—about love.
Fulbert Love. Yes. (*He mutters*)

> "If she would once have pity
> And take me . . ."

He took her from me, you know. Why did he take her from me? He's
tired of her now. He's flung her on the ash-heap at Argenteuil. Is he
going to make a nun of her? Does he think if he makes a nun of her he
can break the marriage and be priested?

Fulbert looks up at the two hooded figures, who move quietly down towards
Guibert

Guibert (*with a little laugh*) I—I never heard the master had any notion of
  Orders. (*His laugh peters out as one of the silent figures nears him*)
Fulbert Why else should he send her to Argenteuil? She's going about in
  her grave-clothes, all but the veil, and they'll put that on her shortly, and
  then he'll be satisfied. He'll take his vows of chastity, and be on his way
  up the ecclesiastical ladder. Are you fond of your master, Guibert?
Guibert Y—yes, your Reverence.

Fulbert So am I. That's why I mean to save his soul. Help me. Between us, Guibert, we'll win him back for God and beat the devil, and Holy Mother Church will be mocked no more, no, nor dragged, scabrous, into the gutter.

Guibert I must be going now, your Reverence. I'll give you back your money, if you don't mind.

The silent figure moves closer

Fulbert (*producing a long purse and weighing it in his hand*) How much do you think there is?

Guibert (*hoarsely*) Fifty? (*He peers at the purse*)

Fulbert A hundred. A hundred gold besants.

Guibert I'll be going, Sir.

The figure sends Guibert sprawling at Fulbert's feet

Fulbert Tell me, is the gate at the foot of the stairs locked at night?

Guibert I must go, Sir, really . . .

Fulbert Suppose you came down the stairs and opened the gate and found this on the steps, what would you do?

Guibert I—don't know.

Fulbert Yes, you do. You'd pick it up and be off into the night and enjoy yourself. Of course, you'd leave the gate *open*, wouldn't you?

Guibert No.

Fulbert Yes, you would. So that you could—get back in.

Guibert (*kneeling up to look fearfully into Fulbert's face*) Master Fulbert, you—you wouldn't *murder* him?

Fulbert (*crossing himself*) No, I hope he'll live long and chaste, the way I would have him. Of course, he won't be a priest. It takes a whole man to be a priest. But he'll live the holier for it. Didn't Our Lord say some have made themselves eunuchs for the Kingdom of Heaven's sake? I doubt Master Peter will ever do that. But I know those who will do it for him. (*He looks up at the still silent figures*)

The figures turn away and pull their cloaks tighter about them

He's a proud man, Peter Abelard. Proud.

The figures move slowly upstage

I'll break his pride and do his soul a service.

The figures look back at Fulbert

Sing, Guibert, sing. (*He produces another gold coin*)

Hypnotized, Guibert sings. The figures start to go

Guibert "Down from the branches fall the leaves . . ."

The lights fade to a Black-out. Fulbert exits in the darkness

Scene 7

Outside Abelard's house. During the night

Silence, darkness. A spotlight comes up between the towers. Two answering owl hoots are heard. A purse of money is thrown from a tower into the centre of the light. Guibert appears out of the darkness, reaches to pick up the purse, looks round to see he is not observed, then exits. Two figures, cloaked and hooded, pass through the light and go into the tower. Another cloaked figure enters, passes through the light, and goes into the tower. The spotlight fades and goes out. There is the sound of wolves howling

Scene 8

Outside Belle Alys'. Later that night

The lighting comes up to show Belle Alys in her turret, kissing and laughing with Alain. Gerard comes upstairs and joins in the love-making. Guibert enters and knocks at the foot of the stairs. Those in the tower disregard the noise. Guibert hammers twice more, and Alys, disgruntled, flings open the window.

Alys Who's there, for God's sake?
Guibert It's me. I've brought the money. Let me in.
Alys (*scornfully*) Oh, no! (*She returns to her clients*)
Guibert I have, I tell you! (*He knocks*) Let me in! Let me in!

Alain leans out

Alain Guibert, go home like a good lad.
Gerard (*leaning out*) Come back tomorrow.
Guibert Tomorrow! I could be dead tomorrow!

Alain closes the window and they both go back to Alys

   Worse, if they—worse! Let me in! Let me in! (*He pounds desperately*)
Alys Get rid of him, Alain.
Alain (*leaning out*) Look, Guibert, here's a whole silver mark for you, if you go home and go to bed. (*He tosses down a coin*)
Guibert (*ignoring it; contemptuously*) Silver? I've got gold.

Alain leans further out

   Gold! Gold! Gold! (*He opens the purse, takes a fistful of coins and throws them at the window. He throws another fistful, then another*)
Alys Mother of God, he's out of his mind. I'd better go down.
Alain You'll go to no madman.
Gerard He's probably stolen it. (*He shuts the window*)
Guibert Alys! Alys!

Alys! (*He sinks sobbing on his knees, the money all round him*)

Robert appears out of the darkness

Robert Who's that? Guibert? (*He stares at the scattered coins*) Don't cry, man. You haven't lost it. I'll help you pick it up. (*He starts to do so*) Gold. Where did you get this?

Guibert Gold. He said gold. The Canon.

Robert Canon? Which Canon? (*Suddenly*) Why aren't you at Master Abelard's— did Canon Fulbert give you this money? What for? (*He shakes him like a rat*) What for??

Metallic spaced clinks are heard, as though knives are being sharpened

Guibert I didn't do it. I only opened the door. Just the door, that's all. I didn't do it.

Guibert breaks away from Robert and runs off

Robert (*suddenly*) Oh dear God, no. (*Crescendo*) Oh, sweet God in Heaven, *no* . . .

Robert hurls himself into the darkness

SCENE 9

Just before dawn

The following happens very quickly

Jehan and the Student rise and exit. Alain runs down the stairs, calling "Gerard! Philippe!" and exits. Philippe and Gerard exit. The Young Whore rises and goes upstage

Four Nuns enter carrying a litter bed with the bedclothes turned back, put it downstage, then stand back on either side. They make a continuous, low-pitched discordant cry

The five Students enter carrying Abelard, naked except for a length of linen cloth. They lay him in the bed. One of the Nuns moves in to remove the cloth and cover Abelard with the bedclothes, then all the Nuns exit

The Students, when they have laid Abelard down, turn upstage and form a line immediately behind the bed. They squat on their haunches, making a continuous, discordant howling noise, which rises in pitch and crescendo to the end of the scene

The lighting fades down, except for a light on Abelard, writhing in the bed, and a silvery night effect on the squatting figures

Robert enters and watches the ensuing scene in the shadows. The Whores watch from upstage, and the two heavily cloaked figures from up C. Guibert enters out of the shadows, muttering incoherently "It wasn't me—I didn't do it." *He comes towards the Students as if drawn, hypnotized, by the sound. As he reaches the waiting group, a Student from each end of the line rises and moves to either side of him. He moves a step back in alarm, but the two Students put an arm out to cut off his escape. A Student from each end of the line rises and moves up towards Guibert. The middle Student, remaining on his haunches, lifts and opens his arms. Guibert steps down towards him. The first two Students seize Guibert's arms, and the middle Student his feet. The other two Students face upstage on either side of Guibert. All lift Guibert in the air, the middle Student kneeling up and opening Guibert's legs wide.*

A spotlight comes up on Guibert. The two Students facing upstage draw knives, hold them out on either side on straight arms. Guibert screams. The Students slowly bring the knives down in an arching movement over Guibert's crotch. On his bed, Abelard writhes in agony.

The lights fade to a Black-out. The clinking sounds stop. A baby cries. In the darkness Guibert is lowered to the ground and exits.

SCENE 10

Abelard's room   **22**

Robert stands in one of the towers, rolling a bandage. Gilles appears in the doorway, staring at Abelard, who is propped up in bed. In the distance Students are heard singing "The Abbot of Angers". The Nuns and Students remain upstage to watch the scene.

Gilles How is he?

Robert Asleep.

Abelard (*in a light brittle voice*) I suppose they've told you that I'm going to live?

Robert takes a beaker of water from the tower shelf, gives Abelard a sip, props him up in bed, then goes and joins the line of Students

What day is it?

Gilles The first of October.

Abelard Three days. "And on the third day . . ." Have they begun to joke yet?

Gilles Not yet.

Abelard I doubt if I'd have had the decency to keep off it so long, if it had been friend Alberic of Rheims, for instance, instead of me. By the way, this must be a high day for Alberic. The first of October. The feast of St Rémy, isn't it? Do you know how they keep the feast at Rheims, Gilles? You go to a church with a raw herring dangling behind you on a string, and the point is to step on the herring of the man in front, and keep your herring from the advances of the man behind. I'd give a good deal to see Alberic's arse taking part in that procession. You're hard to amuse today, Gilles.

Gilles (*dropping his hand on the hand that lies on the coverlet*) Would God
I had died for thee, O Absalom, my son, my son.

There is a silence

Abelard I was lost for you, Gilles.

Gilles I was sick in bed when I heard. And then—I was drunk.

Abelard Yes, they told me. Oh, there's nothing they haven't told me—
Guibert—and the old man, too, dragged from sanctuary. Flesh for
flesh, obscenity for obscenity. I'm glad you came before they move me.

Gilles Where?

Abelard To St Denis.

Gilles If you want monks' nursing, you'd be quieter at St Germain.

Abelard You see, I'm taking the vows at St Denis. Yes, they're making an
exception in my case; it will only be a nominal novitiate. Handsome of
them, I thought.

Gilles (*on his feet, choked*) If I had the power, Peter, I'd put you under
lock and key, till God was pleased to restore you to your senses.

Abelard Having only just removed them, I doubt He'll do that in a hurry.
Do sit down. I can only see your belly and I prefer your face.

Gilles sits again, seething

Of *course* I don't want to be a stupid, sublimating little monk. I've no
vocation. I'd rather continue to teach as I've always done. But that's over.

Gilles You say this because you're sick. When your strength comes back—
when you're your own man again . . .

Abelard I'm nobody's "man", as you so delicately put it, or ever will be.

Gilles Your body's mutilated, not your mind.

Abelard We'll see.

Gilles Good God, man . . .

Abelard That word again.

Gilles I'm sorry. A habit.

Abelard Break it. Go home and read Deuteronomy and Leviticus about the
kind of thing I am now, and then ask yourself how I could go back to run
the Schools. I'd stammer at the first snigger.

Gilles There'd be plenty to choke it down the throat that uttered it.

Abelard Fists are no answer to a jibe.

Gilles I didn't know you were a coward.

Abelard No more did I. But I do now. It's supposed, I believe, to be the
inevitable consequence. No, I've laughed at too many people myself to
stand being laughed at now. I don't say I haven't been jibed at—but so
far I had the sharper tongue of the two.

Gilles Suppose you don't make up your mind now—that you go for a
while to Le Palais . . .

Abelard (*with a cry*) For God's sake! (*After a moment he controls himself*)
No, it has to be. I think I've always known it. I knew it, riding down to
Brittany with—with her. And before, when I went to Fulbert and said
I'd marry her. And before that, long before. Remember when I went to
Laon and read theology? It was a kind of bargain. I thought if I went

one mile I—I wouldn't be asked to go twain. Like Saul on the road to
Damascus. Well, I've been kicking long enough against the pricks, long
enough to be lamed for life, anyhow. Except that Saul saw a great light
before he went blind. I haven't seen—more than the occasional flicker.
Perhaps in time . . . I must say they're making me very welcome at St
Denis. I've never had so many civil things said to me in my life.

Gilles (*bitterly*) They know they'll be the talk of Christendom. What's the
tomb of the kings to putting their cowl on Peter Abelard?

Abelard And they're taking me with no patrimony. I told Abbot Adam I
must make whatever provision I had for—for my wife and son.

Gilles (*after a pause*) Peter, what's to become of Heloise?

Abelard She'll take the veil at Argenteuil.

Gilles (*on his feet again*) What?

Abelard That is, if they'll have her. She'll need to convince your cousin,
the Abbess, she has a vocation. She still has all her faculties. There should
be no problem.

Gilles But she has no vocation!

Abelard Neither have I.

Gilles That's *your* madness. Bury yourself alive if you must—don't bury
her too!

Abelard She's willing.

Gilles Of course she's willing! She'd go through hell if you asked her. But
what right have you to ask?

Abelard (*defiantly*) What else can she do? What kind of world is it for a
woman without kin of her own and a husband, if you can call him that,
in the cloister?

Gilles What's to stop her going to your sister, with the boy?

Abelard Because, if you must have the truth, I couldn't stand it! Because
I couldn't endure even to see her kiss my brother-in-law. Because I'm
jealous of every man that even looks at her! Jealous! Christ, there's
always been jealousy. And that—that was when I was a man myself.
Now . . . (*he is convulsed with emotion, the sobs tearing out of him*)

Gilles Forgive me.

Robert slips in

Robert Master, it's Abbot Adam of St Denis.

Abelard nods

Robert goes

Abelard (*controlled but exhausted*) God bless you, Gilles. But I must go my
own way.

Gilles rises and moves away. The lights fade to a spot on him

Gilles (*after a moment; stirred to his soul*) One goes through life, chewing
the sweet and spitting out the bitter—and then—at an age when one

might reasonably think all heat of the blood were passed—to have the heart torn out of you for two creatures nearly half a century away . . .

He turns away, broken, and exits. The students carry Abelard out. The light fades

SCENE 11

23

The Abbess's room at Argenteuil

There is the voice of a Nun singing the "Dies Irae". The Abbess is seated, with Heloise standing near her. The Nuns are visible through the grill: they all have bare feet

Abbess It came as something of a surprise to me to hear that you wish to enter the religious life.

The Abbess waits. Heloise says nothing.

When I granted your request to wear novice's dress, I understood it was simply a matter of convenience.

Heloise says nothing

You understand that we must be satisfied your vocation is genuine? That there are certain questions I'm bound to ask you?
Heloise Yes, Reverend Mother.
Abbess Very well. (*She indicates a chair beside her*)

Heloise sits

This is your own unprompted desire?
Heloise Yes, Mother.
Abbess You are aware of its meaning? You've considered carefully?
Heloise Yes, Mother.
Abbess When was your vocation revealed to you?

Heloise hesitates

Was it recently?
Heloise Yes.
Abbess Suddenly?
Heloise Yes.
Abbess What caused it? Why do you think God has chosen you to be his handmaiden?
Heloise (*after a moment*) No one can explain God's grace, Reverend Mother. But can whoever receives it doubt that he or she has been led by the hand?

There is a pause

Abbess You are married. You have a son of nine months. You realize, if you are received, the child can no longer remain here with you?
Heloise Yes, Mother.
Abbess What will become of him?

Heloise He will be adopted by my husb—by my sister-in-law.

Abbess You will miss your son?

Heloise Yes—yes, I shall miss him.

Abbess And your husband?

Heloise cannot speak

(*Deliberately*) And your beloved husband?

Heloise And my beloved husband.

Abbess And yet there's no doubt in your mind that your renunciation of your son, your husband, your married life and all that goes with it, is a manifestation of God's grace?

Heloise What else could it be?

Abbess A trick of the devil?

Heloise Surely the devil would not bring me to this decision?

Abbess Why not?

Heloise Because—because it would be to his purpose to leave me in the world, where I might succumb to temptation.

Abbess (*after a pause*) You cannot tell me why God chose you. Can you tell me when all doubt was removed from your mind?

Heloise (*carefully*) I was always conscious of sin—but sin was so delightful in the beginning that I could not withhold myself. But as I continued to sin I became more and more conscious that—that . . .

Abbess That you were losing your soul? That the devil's hand was extended to grip you?

Heloise I don't know that I thought about the devil.

Abbess But we are conscious of sin because we believe in Hell.

Heloise Should we not still be conscious of it if—if Hell didn't exist?

Abbess (*astounded*) Didn't exist?

Heloise I mean, wouldn't it still be possible to—to attain redemption? To atone?

Abbess We atone by confessing our sins to a priest and performing the penance imposed upon us.

Heloise For some this may not be enough.

Abbess Why must you go further?

Heloise My—my conscience tells me I must.

Abbess What if I were to tell you that I believe your conscience to be mistaken?

Heloise I should reply that it is you, Reverend Mother, who is mistaken.

Abbess (*after a pause, intimately*) Heloise, you loved a man. You have a child by him. These ties are strong. They come in the night and call like sirens. Long after one thinks them forgotten, they return in dreams to stir the flesh and distract the spirit. Memory is all-insinuating, all-pervasive. How will you conquer memory, child?

Heloise I—I will pray for strength.

Abbess Then you fear its power?

Heloise Yes—no—I—I was always unhappy about my marriage. As you know, my son was born out of wedlock. It preyed on my mind.

Abbess Surely your marriage soothed your conscience?

Heloise No.

Abbess Why not?

Heloise Because—because I wished—I longed only to be a bride of Christ.

Abbess I see. (*With growing tenacity*) And this wish—this longing—it transcends all things?

Heloise Yes.

Abbess All earthly love?

Heloise Yes.

Abbess All carnal desire?

Heloise Yes.

Abbess It is your reason for asking to be received? Your only reason?

Heloise Mother, are all these questions . . .?

Abbess Your *reason*, child? Your *only* reason?

Heloise Surely it's enough that I . . .

Abbess Your only reason?

Heloise My only reason.

Abbess You long for God? With all your heart and with all your mind and with all your soul?

Heloise Yes. Yes.

Abbess You recognize that, once taken, your decision is irrevocable?

Heloise Yes.

Abbess That you will no longer be able to come and go as you please?

Heloise Yes.

Abbess That this time, once the convent gates close behind you, they close forever?

Heloise Yes.

Abbess That you will be lost to the world?

Heloise Yes.

Abbess You understand these things?

Heloise I understand.

Abbess And to be so lost is your resolve?

Heloise Yes!

Abbess Your aspiration?

Heloise Yes!

Abbess Your delight, your joy?

Heloise Yes! Yes! Yes! Yes! (*She breaks down, sobbing silently but uncontrollably*)

Abbess (*compassionately*) The religious life is not for all of us. Harsh, unsparing, pitiless even, without a vocation it can be a terrible thing. We must be grateful that by God's mercy we have found the truth in time.

Heloise I've always known the truth. I've always known I had no vocation.

Abbess (*gently*) So have I, my dear.

Heloise Help me, Mother.

Abbess You know I will. In any way within my power.

Heloise rises and kneels at the Abbess's feet

Heloise (*steadily*) Mother, I ask to be received into the Sisterhood.

There is a pause, then the light partially fades

Heloise exits in the darkness

The Abbess turns upstage to face the waiting Nuns, all, with hands together, singing the "Dies Irae"   **24**

SCENE 12

The Convent Chapel, Argenteuil

The Nuns are singing, the Abbess waiting

Nuns (*singing*) Dies irae, dies illa, solvet saeclum in favilla, teste David Cum Sybilla. Quantus tremor est futurus, quando judex est venturus, cuncta stricte discussurus. Tuba minum spongeus sonus per sepulchra regionum omnes ante thronum.

Towards the end of the singing a number of Monks enter and take up positions

As the singing finishes an organ and solo soprano voice are heard. The Abbess turns downstage

Heloise, with cropped hair, enters, clothed in a gorgeous robe. With her hands together in prayer she walks slowly centre, pauses as if taking a silent farewell of the world, then turns upstage towards the waiting Abbess and Nuns. Two Nuns at the rear of the group move down to kneel below the Abbess, facing each other. During the last few bars of the music Heloise kneels between the two Nuns. Silence

Abbess My daughter, you are about to enter the Sisterhood of Christ. At this most sacred moment think on Him to whom now and eternally you commit yourself. Love Him, rest your soul in His, and in the silent reaches of your deepest heart, whisper His holy name.

Music starts. Heloise rises slowly and faces downstage

Heloise Peter . . .

The lighting fades to Black-out. The Nuns and Monks repeat "Peter, Peter", in a whisper. The organ and soprano voice are heard again

The Abbess and Heloise exit. Abelard, now in his Abbot's robes, enters and kneels. Heloise re-enters and kneels

The Nuns stand upstage. All face downstage

Scene 13

The Abbey of the Paraclete   **25**

Heloise is kneeling in prayer, close to and facing the audience. She is the Abbess again. Abelard, once more the ageing Abbot, kneels beside her. As the lighting comes up, the "Peter"s fade out, and the music fades also. Silence. Abelard and Heloise cross themselves. Abelard rises. Heloise rises. Abelard makes a move to leave the chapel, but waits for her to go first. She stands looking at him.

Abelard (*gesturing to her to precede him*) Reverend Mother?

Heloise Don't call me that, Peter. I'm not reverend. I'm not a mother—except to these weary, overwatched girls. Nothing has changed for me. I'm older.

Abelard I am older. You are—as I remember. (*He moves to go*)

Heloise Wait. Please. Don't go.

Abelard turns back

(*Making an effort to be matter-of-fact*) I—I hear they burnt your book.

Abelard The "De Trinitate"? Yes, they said it was heretical.

Heloise Was it?

Abelard Of course. Every book ever written about the Trinity is heretical, barring the Athanasian creed, and even that only saves itself by contradicting everything it says as fast as it says it.

Heloise (*laughing spontaneously in spite of herself*) Oh, that's my Peter! (*She checks herself. After a moment*) How absurd. That we should come to this.

Abelard Absurd?

Heloise Two lovers in fancy dress, wondering what to say to each other.

Abelard You find your clothes ridiculous?

Heloise Don't you?

Abelard No. They tell the truth about you.

Heloise You mistake hypocrisy for religion, Peter.

Abelard A hypocrite? That's not your reputation.

Heloise Oh, I do my work. I train the novices as I was trained. I play the game according to the rules. If there's any merit in keeping vows once you've made them, in not being an open scandal to your profession, that perhaps I have. But it's a heathen virtue, not a Christian.

Abelard They say you're a saint.

Heloise laughs

That no beggar comes to the gate but leaves it blessing you: that they bring you wailing children and they're quiet in your arms: they are wounded and your hands make whole.

Heloise I do what any competent nurse could do.

Abelard "Lord, when saw we Thee and hungered and fed Thee, or thirsty, and gave Thee drink?"

Heloise No. No, you mustn't say that. It's not true.

Abelard (*gently*) Has it never occurred to you that it may be true, that you may not know it?

Heloise If I tell you that when I took the veil I committed myself, not to God, but to you in your mutilation—that at no moment in my life did I give myself so passionately to my husband—that it was like a second marriage—that when I lie in my cell you lie beside me—when I sleep, you sleep with me—when I dream, I dream of your arms holding me—that if you asked me I would come to you here, now, this moment—if I tell you that the need for loving never stops—will you believe me?

Abelard (*after a pause*) Tell me, do you believe in God? Do you think there is a God at all?

Heloise Probably not.

Abelard (*after a pause*) Will you pray with me?

Heloise Why not? It's harmless.

Heloise and Abelard kneel. The lights change so that each is in a separate pool

Abelard O Lord who hath brought us together and parted us when and as it pleased Thee, the work which thou didst begin in mercy finish today in a multitude of mercies, and those whom Thou must part for a time in this world, unite forever in the next, O Thou, our hope, our inheritance, our expectation, our consolation, O Lord who art blest forever. Amen.

Abelard rises and moves upstage, facing front. Heloise remains on her knees. The Monks form a semicircle round Abelard, and the Nuns do the same round Heloise. All hum

Heloise A brief glimpse in an empty chapel—and then good-bye for ever. There's nothing to touch God's cruelty, is there? It's quite sublime. Peter? Peter, where are you? Don't leave me! Peter!

All stop humming

Abelard I'll write to her—I'll write—there'll be letters.

Heloise Letters! Can I embrace a letter, hear its heartbeat, feel its warmth? Can I *love* a letter?

The Monks and Nuns continuously chant "Love, love, love . . ."

Abelard Love God. Love God.

Heloise My darling, my darling . . . I would follow him to hell—

The chanting stops

—itself if he asked me, but . . .

Abelard Can it be the one place she won't follow me is Heaven?

Heloise He doesn't know how it is for me. His God has helped him not to want me. He's maimed in soul as well as body, but I . . .

Abelard She thinks because the body fails, desire fails with it. If only it were true.

The Monks give a loud sigh

Heloise Oh, my Peter, you are everywhere still—everywhere.

Abelard And God?

Heloise Nowhere. So what can I expect of God?

Abelard Expect nothing. Give.

The Monks and Nuns repeat continuously "Give, give, give . . ."

Heloise And if one has already given, and there's no more oil in the lamp?

The Monks and Nuns give a sharp shout "Ha!" *The Monks turn to face Heloise*

Abelard I know. I know. When I entered St Denis it was to hide my shame. No other reason. I had no vocation either. For months I was sick in mind and body.

Heloise Warm sweet body.

Abelard And then, when I could get about, I walked. I tramped ceaselessly day after day.

Heloise Warm sweet body in my arms.

Abelard I walked alone, trying to *will* myself to God. No blind ecstasy drove me, but every sentence I'd ever written or spoken passed before me, like a lifetime to a drowning man—

Heloise My man.

Abelard —and in a kind of pomp of abnegation I offered them humbly to God.

Heloise There is no God.

Abelard I went on and on and on until my mind was empty, a vacuum, nothing remained of Abelard. It was the pride of humility, the ceremonial pride of the Roman salute. I waited for some response. There was none.

Heloise There is no God. Love me.

The Monks and Nuns breathe "Ah" *and continue*

Abelard And then one day I was standing looking down at a river, and something in the still, shining surface of it reminded me of a day I'd forgotten, thirty years before.

Heloise I'm young still. Young and full of life. Love me.

Abelard As a boy I'd gone with my father on pilgrimage to St Gildas. It was winter and the wind blew, but standing on the cliff about the point I'd seen a strange silver pathway.

Heloise I want you, Peter.

Abelard It swept round the headland and out to sea. There was no ripple on it.

Heloise I want you now. I need you now.

Abelard It ran against the tide, directly counter to the waves surrounding it.

Heloise I want you at Mass, when prayer should be purest . . .

Abelard My father, standing beside me, was so withdrawn—

Heloise catches her breath

—that for a time I hesitated to ask him what it was.

Heloise And at night . . .

Abelard When I did, he said "It's the will of God."
Heloise In my cell at night . . .
Abelard I'd no idea what he meant.
Heloise In bed, Peter—alone in bed . . .
Abelard Standing there thirty years later, no heavens opened . . .
Heloise (*writhing*) Sometimes the very movements of my body . . .
Abelard I saw no Son of man. I had no vision.

Heloise catches her breath again. The Monks and Nuns stop the "Ah" sound

But in a moment I felt the blood ebbing from my heart.
Heloise The moment before!
Abelard I thought I was going to die.
Heloise The moment before the ecstasy!
Abelard And then—it happened.
Heloise Love's fulfilment! O my darling . . .

The Monks and Nuns start to writhe, slowly, downwards towards the floor

Abelard (*crescendo*) With no warmth of contrition, no passion of devotion, stripped of all human emotion but with every power of my mind, every pulse of my body—I worshipped God.

The Monks and Nuns lie on the floor, prostrated

Heloise (*with a great cry*) You found your crutch.
Abelard (*firmly*) I found the rock. Let the tempest come, it will not shake me. My belief is sure.
Heloise (*after a pause; quietly*) Master, philosopher, man of God—whenever men speak of giants, they'll remember Abelard.
Abelard (*simply, with great tenderness*) If I'm remembered, it will be for this: that I was loved by Heloise.
Heloise Peter Abelard. My husband.

The Nuns rise, repeating crescendo "Husband, husband, husband . . ."

Abelard My sister in Christ.

Heloise rises. Simultaneously the Monks repeat "Christ, Christ, Christ . . ."
The Monks move Abelard, and the Nuns move Heloise, so that he is down-stage, with his back to her

Heloise My husband. My husband, husband, husband! Peter, where are you? I'm drowning! I'm suffocating in Christ!
Abelard Let go! You belong to Him who has conquered the world. Let go!
Heloise Peter, for God's sake come back!

The Nuns repeat "God's sake" until the end of Heloise's line

I'm so alone!
Abelard God is with you.
Heloise There is no God! There is no God!

*The Nuns shout "No—" and the Monks "God—", they shout the words twice,
then all start to sway slowly from left to right, and continue*

Two shattered lives.
Abelard God's mercy.
Heloise Pitiless!
Abelard Purifying. A scorching fire.
Heloise Alone, alone, alone!

The Nuns intone "Alone" between Heloise's words

Abelard Love Him.

The Monks chant "Love Him".

Love Him—as you loved me—to the furthest reach of your shadow.
Heloise Help me, Peter.

Three Nuns alter their chant to "Help me"

Abelard This is your deliverance—and mine. Let go!
Heloise Help me!

*The chanting continues, the Nuns "Alone", "Help me", the Monks "Love
Him", "Christ", all intermingled but each chant in turn being heard through
the general cacophony of sound*

Abelard Holy Jesus, must I break my heart to comfort hers? (*Summoning
all his power*) My Sister, in *your* strength, your intercession, your
innocence, lies what hope I have of heaven. My guilt is in your hands.
Heloise I don't understand, I don't understand!
Abelard My hands are fouled beyond redemption, but yours . . . Pray
for me. Save me. Go to God—for me. For *me*.
Heloise God knows, I would love God for you, if I could.
Abelard Love me for God.
Heloise I can't, I've tried, I . . . (*Suddenly*) What did he say?

*Heloise and Abelard are gradually separated by the grill, which slowly
descends*

Abelard Love me for God. Love me for God. Did she hear?
Heloise (*gradually, as the thought goes home*) Love him for God . . . Dear
Heaven, am *I* his salvation?
Abelard Did she hear?

The Monks and Nuns stop chanting and swaying. There is a sudden silence

Heloise Peter, am I your salvation? Peter?
Abelard (*urgently*) Did she hear? Did she hear?
Heloise (*with a cry, sudden, fearful*) Yes! Yes, I heard, my brother. My
Brother in Christ!

The Monks and Nuns resume swaying silently

Abelard (*falls to his knees*) My wife. My beloved wife. (*He bows his head*)

The light fades on Abelard. The Monks and Nuns stop swaying. Heloise

stretches out her arms and lifts her head, her body forming the shape of a
cross

Heloise (*calmly and clearly, without exaltation but without despair*) O God—
if there is a God—come now.

There is a long, still silence, then the lights Black-out
In the darkness, after a moment, a recorded voice is heard:

Voice On the twenty-first of April, 1142, at the age of sixty-three, Abelard
died and was buried in the crypt of the Abbey of the Paraclete. Twenty-two
years later, on the sixteenth of May 1164, Heloise died and was buried
there also, but not in the same tomb. So they lay for six hundred and fifty
years. In 1814, by order of the Government of the day, their remains were
carried to the cemetery of Pére Lachaise in Paris, where the noblest of the
sons and daughters of France are laid to rest. There their dust was mingled
and buried under a stone plinth, with the words "Abelard: Heloise—
Forever One". And there to this day they lie together.

CURTAIN

FURNITURE AND PROPERTY LIST

ACT I

On stage: 2 towers, to L and R, with steps, gratings and platforms, and a shelf with books

3 grills (flown)
4 black panels
1 panel with dove cut-out
1 panel with Madonna and Child

Off stage: Scene 3

Large carved chair (**Monks**)
Table with platter of chicken, flagon of wine, 2 goblets (**Monks**)
Book (**Heloïse**)

Scene 5

Bench and 2 books, stool, armchair (**Monks**)

Scene 6

Table, 2 stools (**Monks**)

Scene 7

Pile of books, Virgil and Book of Psalms (**Monks**)

Scene 9

Wheeled chair with cushion (**Gilles**)
Tray with jug of wine and goblet (**Jehan**)
Books of Psalms (**Heloïse**)

Scene 10

Bottle of wine (**Heloïse**)
Beaker of water (**Gisella**)
Litter with reading desk, documents, quill pen, book (**Monks** and **Godric**)

Scene 11

Whipping-block and blood effect (**Monks**)
Table (**Nuns**)
Stool (**Robert**)
Whip (**Abelard**)

Scene 12

Gilles' carved chair (**Monks**)
Jug of wine and 2 goblets (**Jehan**)
Book (**Abelard**)
Plate of fish, brown fur rug (**Jehan**)

Scene 14

High altar with candles and cross (**Monks**)
Candelabra and candles (**Monks** and **Nuns**)
Crosses, crozier (**Monks**)

Personal: **Fulbert:** walking-stick

ACT II

On stage: Bench. *On it:* bowl, knife, mushrooms
                 Cradle
                 Gilded branches
                 Pump
                 On tower shelf: beaker of water

Off stage: Scene 1
                    Pail (**Hugh**)
                    Nun's robe (**Denise**)

                 Scene 3
                    Altar (optional) (**Monks**)
                    Cloth, Holy Book, wedding ring, fur cape (**Gilles**)

                 Scene 4
                    Chair (**Nuns**)
                    Table with books (**Nuns**)
                    Book (**Robert**)
                    Bowl of water, shirt, bandage (**Robert**)

                 Scene 5
                    Communion table with chalice and goblet (**Monks**)

                 Scene 6
                    Empty purse (**Guibert**)
                    Coins (**Fulbert**)
                    Purse filled with gold coins (**Fulbert**)

                 Scene 7
                    Purse of gold (**Figure in Tower**)

                 Scene 8
                    Silver mark (**Alain**)

                 Scene 9
                    Litter bed and bedclothes (**Nuns**)

                 Scene 10
                    Chair (**Nuns**)

                 Scene 11
                    Chair (**Monk**)

Personal: **Abelard:** bloom
                 Heloise: sprig of blossom

LIGHTING PLOT

The following is a simplified plot based on the London production. It can, of course, be modified or expanded to suit individual requirements.

ACT I

To open:	Darkness	
Cue 1	**At Curtain rise** *Slow fade-up on Nuns and Abbess, and dove panel*	(Page 1)
Cue 2	**Abelard** goes into pulpit *Bring up lighting on Abelard*	(Page 1)
Cue 3	**Abelard** leaves pulpit *Fade pulpit and dove*	(Page 2)
Cue 4	**Heloise** ". . . stay with me" *Fade light on Abelard*	(Page 2)
Cue 5	**Students** enter *Brighten general lighting*	(Page 3)
Cue 6	At end of Scene 1 *Fade to Black-out*	(Page 3)
Cue 7	At start of Scene 2 *Fade up general lighting to evening effect*	(Page 3)
Cue 8	At end of Scene 2 *Fade to Black-out*	(Page 6)
Cue 9	At start of Scene 3 *Fade up to interior lighting effect*	(Page 6)
Cue 10	**Gilles:** ". . . not much colour" *Fade to dim light*	(Page 11)
Cue 11	**Gilles:** "You're not listening" *Spot on Guibert*	(Page 11)
Cue 12	**Gilles:** "Ah yes" *Black-out*	(Page 11)
Cue 13	At start of Scene 4 *Fade up to moonlight effect*	(Page 12)
Cue 14	Guibert exits *Crossfade from moonlight to interior light on bench*	(Page 14)
Cue 15	**Gilles:** ". . . to their breasts" *Black-out*	(Page 15)
Cue 16	At start of Scene 6 *Fade up to general interior lighting*	(Page 15)
Cue 17	At end of Scene 6 *Black-out*	(Page 17)
Cue 18	At start of Scene 7 *Fade up as Cue 16*	(Page 17)

Cue 19	At end of Scene 7 *Black-out*	(Page 18)
Cue 20	At start of Scene 8 *Fade up as Cue* 18	(Page 19)
Cue 21	**Heloises** "Peter" *Fade to Black-out*	(Page 20)
Cue 22	At start of Scene 9 *Fade up to bright interior lighting*	(Page 20)
Cue 23	**Gilles:** "For pity's sake, out!" *Black-out*	(Page 22)
Cue 24	At start of Scene 10 *Fade up to dim "convent" lighting*	(Page 22)
Cue 25	**Abbess:** "You know the way" *Black-out*	(Page 24)
Cue 26	**Godric** is brought on *Bring up spot on Godric*	(Page 24)
Cue 27	**Heloise** exits *Black-out*	(Page 27)
Cue 28	At start of Scene 11 *Fade up to interior night lighting*	(Page 27)
Cue 29	At end of Scene 11 *Black-out*	(Page 28)
Cue 30	At start of Scene 12 *Fade up to interior lighting*	(Page 29)
Cue 31	**Gilles:** ". . . receive our prayer" *Black-out*	(Page 32)
Cue 32	At start of Scene 13 *Fade up to faint moonlight*	(Page 33)
Cue 33	**Heloise:** "Peter, it's Good Friday" *Black-out*	(Page 34)
Cue 34	At start of Scene 14 *Fade up to Cathedral Cloister*	(Page 34)
Cue 35	**Abelard** embraces **Heloise** *Bring up blaze of light in Cathedral*	(Page 37)
Cue 36	**Abelard** stares at the cross *Lights fade. Bring up spot on Abelard*	(Page 37)
Cue 37	**Congregation:** "Amen. Amen. Amen." *Black-out*	(Page 37)

ACT II

To open:	Dappled exterior sunlight	
Cue 38	**Heloise:** ". . . walking over her grave" *Black-out*	(Page 42)
Cue 39	At start of Scene 2 *Fade up to dim cloister light*	(Page 42)

Cue 40	**Fulbert:** "I won't see anyone" *Bring up spot on Heloise*	(Page 43)
Cue 41	**Fulbert:** "I must— must think" *Black-out*	(Page 43)
Cue 42	At start of Scene 3 *Effect of chill dawn light*	(Page 43)
Cue 43	**Abelard:** ". . . should ring for us" *Black-out*	(Page 45)
Cue 44	At start of Scene 4 *Dim night interior lighting*	(Page 45)
Cue 45	**Heloise** exits *Black-out*	(Page 47)
Cue 46	At start of Scene 5 *Bring up pool of light on Abbess*	(Page 47)
Cue 47	**Heloise:** "Oh, God—not here." *Fade to Black-out*	(Page 50)
Cue 48	At start of Scene 6 *Fade up to shadowy night exterior*	(Page 50)
Cue 49	**Guibert:** ". . . fall the leaves" *Fade to Black-out*	(Page 51)
Cue 50	At start of Scene 7 *Fade up to spot C*	(Page 52)
Cue 51	Figure enters tower *Fade spot to Black-out*	(Page 52)
Cue 52	At start of Scene 8 *Fade up to shadowy night exterior*	(Page 52)
Cue 53	**Robert** exits *Black-out*	(Page 53)
Cue 54	At start of Scene 9 *Fade up to dim dawn lighting*	(Page 53)
Cue 55	**Abelard** is laid down *Fade except for spot on Abelard and a silvery effect on the Students*	(Page 53)
Cue 56	**Guibert** is lifted up *Bring up spot on Guibert*	(Page 54)
Cue 57	At end of Scene 9 *Black-out*	(Page 54)
Cue 58	At start of Scene 10 *Fade up to normal interior lighting*	(Page 54)
Cue 59	**Gilles** moves away *Fade to spot on Gilles*	(Page 56)
Cue 60	**Gilles** exits *Black-out*	(Page 57)
Cue 61	At start of Scene 11 *Fade up to convent lighting*	(Page 57)
Cue 62	**Heloise:** ". . . into the Sisterhood" *Partially fade lighting*	(Page 59)

EFFECTS PLOT

ACT I

Cue 1	At rise of curtain *Monks and Nuns singing (Palestrina)*	(Page 1)
Cue 2	**Fulbert:** ". . . why didn't he wait?" *Bell tolls*	(Page 9)
Cue 3	**Heloise:** ". . . Where does it come from?" *Bell stops*	(Page 10)
Cue 4	**Abbess:** "God the Holy . . ." *Convent bell tinkles*	(Page 22)
Cue 5	**Nuns:** "Amen" *Bell tinkles*	(Page 22)
Cue 6	**Heloise:** "May I see Godric" *Monks and Nuns singing (Palestrina)*	(Page 24)
Cue 7	**Godric:** ". . . latest angel in the making" *Bell tolls*	(Page 26)
Cue 8	**Godric:** ". . . only innocence" *Bell stops*	(Page 26)
Cue 9	**Godric:** ". . . in Donegal . . ." *Repeat Cue 6*	(Page 27)
Cue 10	**Gilles:** ". . . receive our prayer" *Monks and Nuns singing (Palestrina)*	(Page 32)
Cue 11	**Heloise:** ". . . Peter, it's Good Friday" *Cathedral bells peal out. Lessen volume when next scene starts*	(Page 34)
Cue 12	**Gilles:** ". . . but your pride" *Bell fades*	(Page 34)
Cue 13	**Abelard** and **Heloise** embrace *Choir and organ (Victoria Magnificat)*	(Page 37)

ACT II

Cue 14	At rise of curtain *Distant pipe music and bird song*	(Page 38)
Cue 15	**Abelard:** ". . . white and tender as this" *Fade pipe and bird song*	(Page 38)
Cue 16	**Denise:** ". . . hurricane at four months" *Baby yells*	(Page 38)
Cue 17	**Abelard:** "Not sick, is he?" *Baby stops*	(Page 38)

Cue 18	**Heloise: ". . . over her grave"**	(Page 42)
	Single bell tolls	
Cue 19	At start of Scene 3	(Page 43)
	Sound of tinker - jangling pots, etc.; dog barking, then dying away	
Cue 20	At start of Scene 7	(Page 52)
	Owl hoots twice	
Cue 21	At end of Scene 7	(Page 52)
	Wolves howl	
Cue 22	**Robert: ". . . What for?"**	(Page 53)
	Spaced metallic clinks start, and continue through following scene	
Cue 23	At end of Scene 9	(Page 54)
	Metallic clinks stop. Baby cries	
Cue 24	As **Nuns** finish "Dies Irae"	(Page 60)
	Organ and soprano voice singing (Carmina Burana)	
Cue 25	As **Heloise** exits, during blackout	(Page 60)
	Repeat cue 24	

NOTE ON THE MUSIC

In a rapidly changing production such as this, where the scenery is suggested rather than realistic, music is particularly valuable both in establishing the mood and atmosphere of certain scenes and as a bridge or link between them.

"When Summer On Is Stealing" and "The Abbott of Angers" are available in manuscript from Samuel French Ltd.

The recorded music, as used in the London production is listed below.

Wherever the music is not recorded—i.e. certain chants and prayers of the Monks and Nuns still used today in the Catholic Church—it is sung live.

Recorded Music Plot

Effects Cue 1   Palestrina. Deutsche Grammophon Archiv Production: High Renaissance (16th century) Series F, "Palestrina and his school". SAPM 198343 (b)

Side: Improperia. Agnus Dei, commencing at "Ecce Lignum Crucis . . ."

Effects Cue 6   Palestrina. Record as above. SAPM 198343 (a)

Side: Hodie Christus Natus Est. Kyrie Eleison.

Effects Cue 9   Repeat Cue 6

Effects Cue 10   Palestrina. Record as above. SAPM 198343 (b)

Side: Improperia. Agnus Dei, first 45 seconds.

Effects Cue 13   Victoria O Quam. Gloriosa Est Regnum. Choir of St. John's College, Cambridge. ZRG 620

Side 2, band 1, Magnificat Primi Toni, commencing with "Gloria Patri . . ."

Effects Cue 24   Carl Orff. Carmina Burana. Deutsche Grammophon 139362

Side b, band 21, "In Trutina"

Effects Cue 25   Repeat Cue 24

PRODUCTION PLOT

The following is a simplified plot of various moves and effects—mostly concerning changes of furniture between scenes—as used in the London production. They are intended as a guide only, and can be modified according to individual requirements. The cue numbers refer to corresponding numbers in the margin of the text.

1 The dove panel and other panels upstage of the screen are cleared, leaving the screen open. The Students are the "Monks" without cowls and robes.

2 Two Nuns enter with a chair and set it C. Two Monks enter with a table and and set it RC. All four move upstage and watch the ensuing scene.

3 The Monks take off the table and chair.

4 Two Monks enter with a bench and two books which they set in position and then exit.

5 A Monk enters with Abelard's armchair and stool, sets it, and exits. The Nuns move away upstage.

6 Four Monks enter and set the scene and place a table and two stools in position.

7 A Monk enters with a pile of books, a Virgil and a Book of Psalms among them. He puts them on the table, then joins the Nuns.

8 Two Monks strike the table. Then they and the Nuns move upstage.

9 Monks strike the wine tray, bench and stools. The R, L and C, grills are flown in.

10 The C grill is flown out.

11 A Monk enters with a black whipping-board and places it in the tower, together with a mixture to simulate blood on Abelard's back. Two Nuns enter with a table and set it. Robert enters with s stool, sets it, and sits.

12 Unseen by the audience, a Monk in the tower holds out the black whipping-board which protects Abelard's back. When the symbolic whipping starts, a Monk C assumes a Christ-on-the-Cross position; the other Monks and Nuns then prostrate themselves.

13 A Nun enters with Gilles' chair and sets it by the table, then picks up the whip and Abelard's shirt and exits. Other Monks enter and stand upstage. The Nuns exit.

14 Two Monks strike the chair, two strike the table, one strikes the stool and cushion, then all move upstage and are joined by a sixth Monk.

15 During the opening of this scene a high altar with candles is set up C. A cross is suspended over the altar.

16 The grills fly out and the Cathedral blazes with light.

ACT II

17 The Monks with the branches exit. Two Monks strike the bench, pump, etc.

18 For the altar, a permanent part of the set can be used. Otherwise a Monk sets it during the change. Gilles brings on the cloth, Holy Book, ring and fur cape.

19 Two Nuns enter with a chair and set it. Two Nuns set a table with books below the chair. All then exit.

20 Two Nuns move the chair into position for the Abbess. Two Monks strike the table. The side grills fly in. A Communion table with chalice, etc., is set up C.

21 Two Nuns strike the chairs.

22 Two Nuns set a chair R of the bed, and exit.

23 The C grill flies in. A Monk places a chair for the Abess. Another Monk sets a second chair beside it.

24 Two Monks strike the chairs.

25 The "dove" panel is flown in.

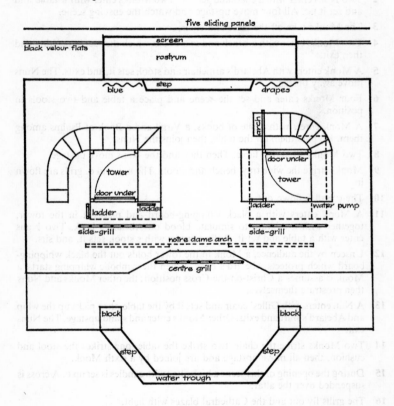